MW00810544

Yearning to Return
Reflections on Yom Kippur

MAGGID

Rabbanit Yemima Mizrachi

Edited by Yikrat Friedman

Yearning to Return
REFLECTIONS ON YOM KIPPUR

Translated by Ilana Kurshan

Parasha VeIsha
Maggid Books

Yearning to Return
Reflections on Yom Kippur

First English Edition, 2019

Maggid Books
An imprint of Koren Publishers Jerusalem Ltd.

POB 8531, New Milford, CT 06776-8531, USA
& POB 4044, Jerusalem 9104001, Israel
www.maggidbooks.com

Original Hebrew Edition © Yemima Mizrachi and
Yikrat Friedman, Parasha VeIsha, 2018
English Translation © Koren Publishers Jerusalem, 2019
Translation of "My Longing, My God, Is for You"
© Abigail Denemark Ossip, 2018

Parasha VeIsha offers more of Rabbanit Yemima Mizrachi's lessons
online, free. For more enriching, spiritual content, visit www.parasha.org

ISBN 978-1-59264-528-2, *hardcover*

A CIP catalogue record for this title is
available from the British Library

Printed and bound in Israel

In memory of my father and teacher
whose soul departed in purity
on the 23rd of the month of Cheshvan 5778
and who took his leave from this world in peace.

לעילוי נשמת

אברהם בן יחזקאל ז״ל

נלב״ע ו׳ סיון תשס״ט

תנצב״ה

הונצח ע״י בני משפחתו

❧

Contents

Part II: Praying with Transgressors

Part III: Human Relations as the Avoda Service

Part IV: With Hand on Heart

Part V: Enveloped in Mercy

Part VI: Approaching Atonement
Customs and Spiritual Practices for Erev Yom Kippur

Part VII: When Entering and Exiting the Holy

Introduction

Never were there more joyous days for the people of Israel than the fifteenth of Av and Yom Kippur, for on these days the maidens of Jerusalem used to go out dressed in white garments – borrowed ones, in order not to cause shame to those who did not have their own.... The maidens of Jerusalem would go out and dance in the vineyards, saying: Young men, lift up your eyes and behold whom you are about to choose for yourself. Regard not beauty alone, but rather consider a virtuous family, for "gracefulness is deceitful and beauty is vain" (Proverbs 31:30).

Mishna Taanit 4:8

The mishna in Taanit teaches that the most joyous days on the Jewish calendar are the fifteenth of Av and Yom Kippur. On both of these days, a woman yearns to return. She yearns for a response in return from the man she seeks, and she yearns for the return back to God. These are the two days in which the verse "I have found the one that my soul seeks" (Song of Songs 3:4) resounds in the open air.

On Yom Kippur, we ask God to seal our names in the book of life, like the seal the lover seeks in the Song of Songs: "Set me as a seal upon your heart, as a seal upon your arm, for love is as fierce as death" (3:4).

On these two days we ask to lift up and to be uplifted. On the fifteenth of Av the maidens say, "Young man, lift up your eyes and behold whom you are about to choose." And on Yom Kippur we pray in the *Ne'ila* service, "We implore you, please, O God, lift up in forbearance, forgive."

These are two days of abundant love, perhaps the greatest festivals on the Jewish calendar. On these two days we achieve closeness by forging paths of connection to one another. Only when we forge these paths and atone for our trespasses will we be able to pave the way to the union of bride and groom, to the union of the Holy One, blessed be He, and the Divine Presence, to a great love that emanates from shattered tablets.

These are two days with mortal stakes, days on which the account ledgers are opened, days on which there is no man or woman, young or old, who does not yearn to return to God and to receive the response that God gave to Moses after the shattering of the tablets: "I have forgiven, as you requested" (Num. 14:20).

Over the course of the year we continue to question and doubt one another's virtues, which makes it impossible to return. We cannot return with these questions still open; we can only return in responsiveness to one other. The time has come, once and for all, for the people of Israel to stop demanding an accounting from one another, and to start holding ourselves accountable to God.

We are allowed to ask questions, but it is far more important to yearn for a response in return, because returning is the overture of love.

This book may be regarded as a collection of all the questions that are forever being asked. It is not a textbook about returning to God in repentance. It need not be read from start to finish. Wherever you open the book, the gates of repentance will open before you.

As we say in the *Ne'ila* prayer, "The day will fade. The sun will set and be gone. We will come in through Your gates." The book is an attempt to find our way in. Together, we will try to forge a path to forgiveness before the hour when the gates are locked.

As we recite in the afternoon service on Yom Kippur, we have come to a place of fire, flare, and flame. And many waters cannot extinguish this love.

Hineni. Here I stand, deficient in deeds, yearning to return alongside you.

Yemima Mizrachi
Jerusalem, Elul 5778

Part I

Bearing Iniquity

My Longing, My God, Is for You

Rabbi Avraham ibn Ezra[1]

My longing, my God, is for You
    My desire and love is for You
My heart and innards are Yours
    My soul and breath are Yours.
My arms and legs are Yours,
    My character is from you.
My bones and blood are Yours
    My skin and my body

---

[1]   Translated by Abigail Denemark Ossip, with advisory support from Dr. Jonathan Decter, https://www.abbiedoespiyyut.com/Lecha Eli Teshukati t.html.

My eyes and thoughts are Yours
>   My shape and my form
My spirit and strength are Yours
>   My trust and my hope is You
My heart, blood, and fat are Yours
>   Like the sheep I sacrifice, my offering
To You, the One with no second
>   My only soul will acknowledge You
Yours is kingship, majesty Yours
>   My praise befits You
Help in troubled times comes from You
>   Be my help in the time of my trouble
My hope when I tremble is to You
>   When I sigh like a woman giving birth
I hope to You, heal my fracture
>   My pain and my wounds
I long, without quieting, for You
>   Until You illuminate my darkness
Eternity is Yours, I trust in You
>   My strength is You
I call to You, I cling to You
>   Until I return to my land
While I still live I am Yours
>   And even after my death

I admit and confess before You
>   For my sins and my wickedness
My salvation is Yours, forgive my wickedness
>   My crimes and my guilt
I bow and spread my hands to You
>   Please hear my supplication
I cry with a downtrodden heart to You
>   With my many complaints and my grief
Kindness is Yours, mercy Yours
>   Have mercy on all my hardship
My sin is too great to bear
>   My lapses too large
Therefore my pains are great
>   My planting falls short
And alas! Woe is me
>   If You judge me according to my wickedness
My inclination is my constant enemy
>   Like an adversary against me
I was advised and tempted by it
>   With devices toward my evil ways
To Him, and none but Him
>   My anger and complaints
And when into my heart ascend
>   My sins, as I lie in bed

I am afraid, I tremble too
> My confusion increases

I am agitated when I mention
> My sins before You

I stand naked before You
> What will my answer be

On the day my deceptions testify against me
> I will eat the fruit of my actions

The days of payment will come
> The time of punishment draws near

When I hear your tidings
> I quake and fear very much

Who can stand before You
> And who can be my exchange

How can I give an account to You
> How can I be righteous in my claim

I am ashamed and I have ambushed
> I have betrayed and I am scorned

I have stolen and I have robbed
> I have become evil and wicked

I have also been rebellious and corrupt
> I have sinned and caused others to sin

I have strayed and I have advised wrongly
> I have deceived and I have denied

I have mocked and I have scorned
    I have rebelled and I have defied
I have spurned and committed adultery
    I have been stubborn and I have exceeded limits
I have distorted and caused distortion
    I have sinned and I have become blemished
I have been hostile and I have caused pain
    I have cursed and I have gone wrong
I have been evil and I have been corrupt
    I have been abominable and made mistakes
And I have left your path
    And my shame has covered me
I have increasingly done evil
    And continued in my evilness
And I have lied and I have been treacherous
    I have extorted and I have oppressed
I sinned at my beginning
    And I was evil at my end
I was guilty in my youth
    And I rebelled in my old age
I have loathed Your teachings
    And have chosen my own teachings
I have abandoned Your will
    And I have followed my desire

I have fulfilled my inclination's will
    And I have not considered my end
I have added many sins
    To my wickedness and my guilt
Therefore my face is covered
    By my shame and my embarrassment
I have no refuge but You
    My forgiveness comes from You
There is no pardoner but You
    My pardon comes from You
If You bring Your servant to judgment
    What is my might worth
What am I, what is my life,
    What is my strength and my power
Like blowing chaff driven away
    How will You remember my mistakes
I have become mute and ashamed
    And my shame has covered me
I will always ask for Your favor
    To grant my requests
And wash me thoroughly
    From my iniquities and my sins
See my great distress
    And my helplessness in my exile

Please do not hide Your ear
     From my sighing and crying out
Your servant is also an advocate for good
     Please say "Enough" to my troubles
Show me Your salvation
     Before the day I die
And the day I fall into my enemies' trap
     Support me in my falling
My soul is sated with wormwood
     Making me weary of my life
Display for me a sign for good
     And rise to my aid
For You are my portion
     My joyful cry and my good
My fate and my praise
     All my joy and happiness
My heart's exultation, the light of my eyes
     My strength and my desire
My rest and my delight
     My quietness and my serenity
Teach me to understand Your service
     My service will be to You
Return to me and I will return
     And You will desire my repentance

Show me Your ways
    And straighten my path
And You will hear my prayer
    And You will answer my supplication
I have sought You wholeheartedly
    Answer me, God, with what I seek
I pour out my tears to You
    Wipe away my sins as I cry
My soul says, "My portion
    God is my inheritance"
Please gather up my sins
    In Your kindness on the day I am gathered up
And the day I walk before You
    Please accept my walking
And with those who do Your will
    Place the reward for my actions
And send the angels of favor
    And let them go out to me
And they will say, "Come in peace"
    With one voice when I arrive
Let them bring me to Your Garden of Eden
    And let my dwelling be there
And I will enjoy Your light
    And place my honor in my resting place

The light hidden before You
     Will be my protection and my shelter
And under the shade of Your wings
     Please give me my place.

Wander the Streets

"Wander the streets of Jerusalem," says the prophet. "If you can find but one person who seeks faith, I will forgive the city" (Jer. 5:1).

This verse is a reminder of an aspect of Yom Kippur that is generally overlooked. Master of the Universe, I hereby proclaim before You that every year during the week before Yom Kippur I wander the streets of Jerusalem and the streets of Tel Aviv and the streets of countless other cities, and what I discover is nothing short of wondrous. You look for one person who seeks faithfulness? I see sanctuaries filled to the brim. People gather; they make their way from lectures on spirituality to *Selichot* services, and the streets of the city resemble a great big pajama party. Everyone is out in the streets, men and women alike, and what are they all searching for? Faith. Everyone shares the same aspiration, and everyone inclines their heads toward the same heaven. And we too seek faith, because there is nothing greater. As the prophet teaches, so long as the people have faith, God will forgive the city.

Rabbi Levi Yitzchak of Berditchev (1740–1809) frequently emphasized this point in his ardent words about his fellow Jews. Several stories about Rabbi Levi Yitzchak take place on the eve of Yom Kippur, with the whole community gathered in the synagogue awaiting the arrival of their rabbi to begin the *Kol Nidrei* prayer. Here is one story of many:

> It happened once that Rabbi Levi Yitzhak came to the beit midrash on the night of Yom Kippur. He paced to and fro, but did not begin the recitation of Kol Nidrei. At the same time, he noticed a man sitting on the ground in the corner, crying.
>
> Rabbi Levi Yitzhak said to him, "Why do you cry so?"
>
> The man replied: "Rabbi, how can I not cry? Yesterday I had everything, and today I am forlorn,

and lacking everything. Lest the rabbi think that I did not behave properly, it is not so. I sat in my village, and whoever came to my door, I gave him food and drink, and whoever came to me hungry went away satiated. And my wife would behave with even more kindness than I. She would walk around the village to see if there was anywhere a poor Jew who needed to be fed.

"And now, the One above came and took my wife from me, and she died. And if this were not enough, He burned down my house, so that I am left bereft of my wife and with no home. And I have six small children. I also had a large siddur with all the *piyyutim* (liturgical poems) and prayers marked so that I did not have to turn the pages to find a single prayer. This too was burned. So how can I forgive Him?"

Immediately, the rabbi ordered him to search the *beit midrash* for a similar siddur. He searched and found one. The man sat and turned page after page to see if this siddur was ordered like the one that had been burned. It took him about an hour, and during that entire time the rabbi stood and waited.

Finally the rabbi said to him, "Now can you forgive God?"

The man answered, "Now I can forgive Him."

Then the rabbi approached the pulpit and began to recite *Kol Nidrei*.[1]

This story moves me to tears, because so many men and women have lost their faith after suffering loss. Rabbi Levi Yitzchak of Berditchev explains that yes, there are losses that cannot be restored. It is impossible to bring back a father or mother. People suffer loss and they lose faith. But if they have a prayer book, then they have a way of connecting with God, and they can forgive God for their losses. They can plead with God, "Do not cast me out of Your presence, or take Your holy spirit away from me" (Ps. 51:13).

"Will the prayer book bring you comfort?" Rabbi Levi Yitzchak asked that Jew, because the prayer book represents our connection with God. "The prayer book

---

1   From Simcha Raz, *Loving and Beloved: Tales of Rabbi Levi Yitzhak of Berdichev, Defender of Israel* (Menorah Books, 2016).

brings me comfort," the man responded, and then the Yom Kippur prayers could begin.

All of us have suffered losses in the year that has passed. But we must not lose our connection with God as well. We must plead with God to remain inside of us. We must cry out, "Let me again rejoice in Your salvation" (Ps. 51:14).

During the Ten Days of Repentance, we are like sleep-walkers in the night, all seeking connection. Each year I see so many people who are trying to connect to God. There are so many women who come to my classes in search of religious connection. No one asked them to show up. They were drawn by their own yearning to rejoice in a connection with God once again.

Returning Again

Sometimes it seems as if on Yom Kippur we suffer from a lack of credibility. After all, we have already stood before God and said, "We have sinned, we have transgressed." We asked forgiveness, and then we went right back to sinning. This is what we did last year, and the year before that…. And so what is the point of this ritual, if we're just going to lapse again?

Rabbi Tzvi Elimelekh Shapiro of Dinov (1783–1841), the author of *Bnei Yissaskhar*, explains in a magnificent parable that the purpose of Yom Kippur may be compared to a uniquely feminine capacity. "Like a woman drawing close to childbirth, she writhes and cries out in her pangs – so are we become because of You, O Lord"

(Is. 26:17). Consider a woman in childbirth. Right after she gives birth, she swears, "I never want any more children!" She must therefore bring a sin offering (Nidda 31b). But then she is overcome by desire once again, and once again, unabashedly, she writhes and cries out in her pain. She will renege, get pregnant, give birth, and once again cry out in her pain, "Enough! No more!"

This image transports us back to Eve's curse in Genesis: "And to the woman He said: I will greatly increase your sorrows and your pregnancies" (Gen. 3:16). As the *Bnei Yissaskhar* notes, something seems out of order here. A woman's pain begins with pregnancy, and only then does she experience the sorrow of raising children. First comes the desire for her husband, then pregnancy and childbirth. But it's more complicated than that. After she gives birth, she longs to get pregnant again, even though during her previous labor she cursed and swore, "I will never get pregnant again." "And your desire shall be for your husband" (Gen. 3:16), in spite of the pain. Sorrow precedes pregnancy, but it does not preclude it.

Why does a person draw close to God, only to grow more distant? Because between one slip and another, between one more sin and one more sacrifice, something is born. A baby is born. "And he," the husband, "will rule over you." He will learn the rules from his wife when he repents before the Holy One, blessed be He, "like a woman drawing close to childbirth." The renewed force of women's desire drives the wheels of repentance in the world.

The woman, too, is not the same woman. A new conscience has been birthed, and now she recoils from sin and seeks out the Holy One, blessed be He. God looks at her renewed desire, her cyclical longing, and He says to her: Can I deny your wishes, when you return to Me this way? "And he will rule over you," says the *Bnei Yissaskhar*. God will learn the rules from her. And He will say: I want you too. "I am my beloved's and his desire is for me" (Song of Songs 7:11).[1]

Anyone who thinks that he remains the same person after Yom Kippur is making a grave error. Because even if we go astray yet again, every Yom Kippur elevates us as human beings. Something is born inside us after all

---

[1] See Rabbi Tzvi Elimelekh of Dinov, *Bnei Yissaskhar*, Tishrei essays, 6.

that repentance and remorse. We will sin again, but it will be different, because we are different. We have pangs of conscience. We have a deeper understanding of the sins we committed. We are never the same again.

If so, our Sages have bequeathed to us the understanding that women, and femininity, have an astounding influential force, particularly during the Ten Days of Repentance. It is specifically the most powerful feminine capacities that have the potential to lead all of Israel into a happy new year. Foremost among them is the capacity for birthing, and its attendant longing, which is renewed between sin and repentance. It is not just a new year that is born.

Don't Be Sad
That You Feel Bad

Every September my inbox is flooded with urgent pleas: "Yemima, I'm so disgusted with myself. I promised myself that I wouldn't repeat the same behavior patterns, but it keeps happening. No matter how much I regret it, I keep doing it." I could not possibly convey all the remorseful messages that fill my inbox in the weeks leading up to Yom Kippur.

Rabbi Shlomo Wolbe (1914–2005) wrote that when a person's remorse becomes so intense as to inspire a sense of disgust with herself (not to mention a note to Yemima Mizrachi!), the Holy One, blessed be He, regards the pain she feels in sinning as part of her punishment and atonement. If a person sighs during the very act of sinning, it is recorded in heaven that "so-and-so sinned, but while sighing." If a person does not sigh while sinning, it is recorded in heaven that "so-and-so sinned without sighing."[1] The difference is enormous. Sighing is a sign of remorse. After we experience remorse, we may still transgress, but we will do so without the desire for sin.

When a person sighs, a sense of disgust takes root, and this in itself diminishes the desire to repeat the same patterns. After all, what is repentance? It is about returning to the same situation where we once sinned. We're with the same people, in the same place, but this time we're no longer so excited about the prospect of sinning. According to Rabbi Yonatan Eybeschutz (1690–1764), each time we find ourselves in this same situation, we should know that we have the opportunity to turn back.

As Maimonides writes, "What is repentance? It is when the sinner abandons his sin and rids his thoughts of it and resolves in his heart that he will not do it again,

---

1 Rabbi Shlomo Wolbe, *Alei Shur* [Hebrew], part II, 440–441.

as it is written, 'Let the wicked abandon his ways' (Is. 55:7). And he will regret that he sinned, as it is written, 'Now that I have turned back, I am filled with remorse' (Jer. 31:18)." Then, Maimonides explains, "The One who knows all secrets will testify that he will never return to the same sin."[2]

After we repent, we will never sin in the same way again, because we will lose some of that desire. We may commit the same sin, but we will be disgusted with ourselves as we do so. We will sin, but with pangs of conscience.

What happens to all that desire? Desire never disappears. It is just the object of desire that shifts. "My longing, my God, is for You." One of the thirteen attributes of God is that He is "bearing iniquity" (Ex. 34:7). If we want God to bear our sin, we have to give up our sin for God. We can't just dismiss it as insignificant, or say that everyone else does it too. We have to make a big deal of it, which may even involve writing a note to Yemima Mizrachi saying, "I hate myself, I'm disgusting, I did it again." Each time I receive a message like this, I regard it as the first step to repentance.

---

2   Maimonides, Laws of Repentance 2:2.

23

Once we give up our sin for God, we are filled with disgust and remorse, and our desire to serve God will necessarily be redoubled. We've given up our sin. We've suffered a loss. We were in a place of great darkness. How then will we not roar unto God like the roar of the sea?

We Are Truly Angels

In the ten days between Rosh HaShana and Yom Kippur, we try to act as best we can. Sometimes it's hard not to mock ourselves for our newfound piety: "Since when am I so devout?" But according to the Seer of Lublin (Rabbi Jacob Isaac Horowitz, 1745–1810), it is really a voice within ourselves that is deceiving us. This inner voice leads us to think that our return to God in the months of Elul and Tishrei is all just an act we put on. But the truth is that the way we behave in Elul and Tishrei reflects our true essence. It is throughout all the rest of the year that we are putting on an act.

These days are authentic. We are our true selves. Whether we come to synagogue on Yom Kippur by bicycle or Ferrari, it's all authentic. There is an authentic impulse to fulfill one more commandment, to catch at least one small part of the prayer service. The devoutness that we discover within is genuine.

In the Bible God says of Yom Kippur, "For on this day atonement shall be made for you to purify you of all your sins. You shall be purified before the Lord" (Lev. 16:30). The talmudic Sages comment that it is the essence of the day that purifies (Yoma 85b). It is not "on this day," but rather "by means of this day." By means of this day, God forgives us. The essence of Yom Kippur cleanses and purifies and changes us. The very fact that we have gone through the day means that it has done its work on us, as if we have passed along on a conveyor belt through a purifying machine.

The most definitive moment of the year takes place at the end of Yom Kippur, immediately following the blowing of the shofar at the conclusion of the _Ne'ila_ prayer. At this point, everyone simply blesses one another. The blessings we offer one another at the end of the fast have a special force, because they are recited with pure lips – lips that have recited the confessional prayer and the thirteen attributes of God's mercy from the depths of the heart. Bless and be blessed.[1]

The Hebrew word for absolution, *mechila*, comes from the same root as the word for dance, *machol*. Perhaps it should not come as a surprise that hasidic Jews used to break out in dance at the end of Yom Kippur. It is a moment of supreme joy – the joy we have dreamed of our whole lives.

The Rebbe of Kobryn offers the following parable. Imagine that you are in great debt. You take out yet another loan. And another. Then the bank manager calls and summons you for a meeting. You arrive in fear and trembling and he sits down across from you with an itemized list of all your debts.

"Are you responsible for all of these?" he asks you, looking over the list.

"Well…"

"Do you have a way of paying them off?"

---

1   Rabbi Wolbe, *Alei Shur*, part 1.

"Well…no."

"Do you want to keep living this way, sinking into greater and greater debt?"

"No."

"Well then I'm canceling all your debts," he announces.

What a shock. After all, what do we ask of God on Yom Kippur? "Our Father, our King, erase in Your abundant mercy all records of our sins." God restores our bank balance to zero, allowing us to start all over again.

Yom Kippur is a wondrous creation. It is God's masterpiece. As we read in the book of Psalms, "All the days created for me were written in Your book, save one of them" (139:16). God creates all our days, and each day is furnished with its desires and impulses – the good impulse and the evil impulse. But there is one day when the evil impulse is powerless over us. On this day nothing stands in the way of abundant goodness. This day changes everything. It's a day that finds us all looking white and beautiful. We all become angels, riding our angelic chariots with wheels (or our two-wheeled bicycles). Where did all this beauty come from?

It is the beauty of our true selves, devoid of the evil impulse.

Maimonides writes that every individual must repent until "the One who knows all secrets will testify that he will never return to the same sin."[2] What does it mean that God will testify for us? Rabbi Yosef Karo (1488–1575) explains in the *Kesef Mishne* that the individual calls God in to testify for him. He invokes a verse from Hosea: "Return, Israel, unto the Lord your God" (14:2). The Hebrew word for unto, *ad*, may be vocalized so that it instead reads "witness," *eid*. According to Rabbi Karo, Maimonides maintains that on Yom Kippur, God is called in as a witness to testify to our true desire to be better and more authentic people. Our newfound piety is genuine. It is nothing but the truth.

---

2   Maimonides, Laws of Repentance 2:2.

Beginning to Hope Again

Elul is a period of discovering what we yearn for most. Throughout the month of Elul our dreams and wishes guide us like a lighthouse beacon: *I am my beloved's, and my beloved is mine. It is my beloved I yearn for above all!*

Rosh HaShana is like a first date. Girl meets guy, and she realizes that he's what she wants. "This is it," she says. The difference between Elul and the Ten Days of Repentance is that the former is a period of dreams, whereas the latter is a period of desire. The Ten Days of Repentance are not just about penance, but also about pining. The woman realizes, "This is really happening. I can't mess it up now." She walks around in a daze, confused about what she is supposed to be doing.

She makes up with others. She makes herself up anew. She removes her makeup and then reapplies it, more heavily this time…

She knows that every detail is critical, and she chooses her words carefully. During the Ten Days of Repentance there are several additions to the prayer service: "Remember us for life," "Who is like you, compassionate Father," "the holy King." If she forgets and accidentally says "the holy God" as on the rest of the year, then she has to return to the beginning of the prayer and say it again, correctly this time: "the holy King." Why? She doesn't ask why. A woman in love does not ask why. She knows that everything has to be done just so.

It is for this reason that people flock from all over the country to attend lectures and classes about Yom Kippur. I prepare brilliant insights and sophisticated ideas, and then I realize that I am standing in front of a room of exhausted women who have come from near and far. I say to myself, "Enough, Yemima. Keep it simple. Touch people. Everyone has come to your lecture because they are in love, because this is what they fervently wish for, because they simply can't let themselves miss out on this opportunity." In the midrash the word for desire, *teshuka*, is explained as a combination of *tasha*, weakening, and *mekava*, hoping.[1] After a period of tremendous weakening, a woman begins to hope again.

God will send countless signs of His love when He is so close. Suddenly we encounter all sorts of people we've been meaning to ask forgiveness from for a long time. God sends them our way, because we are in the midst of a giant pajama party, wandering the streets in the night, seeking faith, searching for forgiveness.

In Sephardic synagogues the Yom Kippur prayers begin with the liturgical poem by Ibn Ezra quoted earlier:

> My longing, My God, is for You
> My desire and love is for You
> My heart and innards are Yours
> My soul and breath are Yours.

Creator of the Universe, You know that we have sinned and stumbled. We have strayed, we have wandered in strange pastures. But what do we truly yearn for? Only You. A new desire has been born inside us – our desire and love is for You.

---

1   See the *Etz Yosef* on Genesis Rabba 20:7.

The Shattered Tablets of a Broken Heart

Rabbi Yechiel Michel Epstein (1829–1908), author of the *Arukh HaShulchan*, writes, "Yom Kippur atones only for those who believe in its atonement."[1] This is quite a trenchant remark. If we don't believe that every Yom Kippur has left its mark on us, then we have missed out on the entire essence of the day, and there is really no point in taking part in it.

But what if we really don't believe it? According to rabbinic tradition, it was on Yom Kippur that Moses

---

1 *Orach Chayim* 607.

descended the mountain with the second set of tablets. Forty days earlier he shattered the first set of tablets bearing the Ten Commandments after he observed the people dancing around the Golden Calf. On Yom Kippur he returns to the people, bearing the news of God's extraordinary forgiveness. Suddenly they see that there is a second set of tablets. There is a second chance.

The whole nation breaks out in tears upon catching sight of the new set of tablets. They wonder, "Can it really be? After all, the first set of tablets, which Moses shattered, were like a marriage contract. Do we really get a second chance at love?"

But there is one woman who stands amid the people and thinks, "He's returned. But not to me." She is Zipporah, Moses's wife, for whom the revelation at Sinai was not a marriage but a separation. According to the midrash, when Moses went up the mountain to receive the Torah, he separated from his wife. Moses became a man of God, a man who belonged wholly to God, a man who was no longer bound in marriage to a woman. At this singular point in history, the Holy One, blessed be He, agreed to such an arrangement. And so Moses left Zipporah.

And now he is returning, in radiant splendor. I imagine her standing there wondering, "But what can I hope for now that he has left me? Will a vessel that was used for holy purposes now be used for the mundane?[2] How can there be anyone else for me after Moses? How can anything good possibly ever happen to me again?"

Heartbroken, she watches as Moses makes his way toward her, with all the people watching him, bearing a ring in his hand.

Moses carved this ring out of the leftover stone from the second tablets, which, according to the midrash,[3] were made of very rare precious stones. God told him, "Carve out for yourself" (Ex. 34:1). The Hebrew word for carve, *pesol*, comes from the same root as the word for waste, *pesolet*, suggesting that God was telling Moses to keep the leftover stone for himself.[4] Moses said to Zipporah, "I carved this ring for you. I carved out space for our marriage. I am bringing you the chronicles of all I've experienced, bound up in this ring."

---

2   See Bava Metzia 84b.
3   See Rashi on Ex. 34:1; Leviticus Rabba 32:2; *Midrash Tanchuma* on *Parashat Ki Tisa* 29:3; *Pirkei DeRabbi Eliezer* 46:3.
4   Rashi on Ex. 34:1.

The words spoken under the wedding canopy ring out for the first time on that historic Yom Kippur: "Behold, you are sanctified to me with this ring in accordance with the law of Moses and Israel." Moses comes bearing the news that even after a weakening of desire, and even after all the letters have flown up to heaven and the parchment of the marriage contract has burned, the letters can be restored and a new ring can be carved. This is the law of Moses. There is no other.

The *Tanna DeVei Eliyahu* vividly depicts the moment of Moses's return:

> On the last day,
> They arose and stood before Mount Sinai
> Crying before Moses
> And Moses cried before them
> Until their crying rose up to the heavens.[5]

I can just hear Moses crying, "I'm coming, I'm coming," and the people crying in greeting. At that moment God's mercy flowed down to Israel and the divine spirit brought good tidings. The Holy One, blessed be He,

---

5   *Tanna DeVei Eliyahu Zuta,* 4.

36

said to Israel: "My children, if you believe in this day, I swear by My great name, by the throne of My glory, that your crying today will become joy and gladness, and this day will be one of joy and gladness, and atonement and forgiveness, and good tidings for you and for your children and for your children's children for all generations."

Every year on the eve of Yom Kippur, Moses is supposed to descend again with the second set of tablets in his arms. Every Yom Kippur we are overcome by that same anxiety and that same terrible sense of abandonment. We hear the whisper in our ears: "Forget it. They have already been shattered a thousand times. There's no way to repair them again. There's no second chance."

But there is a second chance. The tablets and the broken tablets were placed in the ark side by side. This is what we cry for on the eve of Yom Kippur, when we plead with God to grant us a new start. To turn over a new leaf.

Yom Kippur atones only for those who believe in its efficacy. It is not too late. The second tablets rest in the ark beside the first. We can still awaken desires that have been dormant. We can still reach out again to a beloved we thought was lost to us forever.

We must not give up on Yom Kippur.

Rising Dough and
Raising Children:
On Bread and Beginnings

It is customary to bake challa during the Ten Days of Repentance. Upon baking challa, part of the dough is separated in commemoration of the portion that God commanded to set aside for the priests.

It all began in the beginning. On Rosh HaShana, immediately after the world was created, Eve "ruined the world's challa" (Genesis Rabba 17). Adam is referred to as challa because he was formed when God took dust and water and kneaded them together like dough. God breathed the spirit of life into Adam's nostrils and gave him eternal life in the Garden of Eden. And then the snake came along, and Eve was seduced, and Adam ate from the forbidden fruit. From that point on, they, and we, entered a parallel world in which good and evil are mixed up with one another. A world of toil, sweat, and tears.

Imagine that a woman's challa dough is ruined by her neighbor. She makes the perfect dough, and then her neighbor comes along and dumps in a cup of salt. Then imagine what it was like when God's firstborn son was ruined. Someone came over to this child and said to him, "You're so innocent. There are a few things your father has kept from you that you might want to know. Have a look at this Tree of Knowledge. Come taste something you've never tasted before."

If someone were to ruin a child, would the parents not grow furious? If someone were to share inappropriate knowledge or an inappropriate photograph with a child, would the parents not be deeply distressed? Consider the enormous distress of the Creator, whose child was ruined.

But if a person can be ruined, that person can also be reformed. By preparing the dough out of flour and water, we are transported back to the creation of Adam out of water and earth. And by separating a portion of the dough, we redress part of this great despoiling. Thus the kabbalists maintain that the recitation of the Grace after Meals, too, has special spiritual force during the Ten Days of Repentance.

It is possible to bake something entirely fresh with nurturing and caressing hands that braid instead of upbraiding. It is possible to raise a child while the dough rises, and it is possible for a spoiled girl to become well bred. Such a girl can be brought back into the tent of her mothers, even if the candle has gone out and the dough has spoiled and the pure white cloud seems to have drifted away long ago.

Even after great loss, peace may be restored. After Isaac's world fell apart with his mother's death, he met Rebecca, and the flame was rekindled: "Isaac brought her into the tent of his mother Sarah…and he loved her. And Isaac was comforted after his mother's death" (Gen. 24:67). Suddenly the delicious aroma of freshly baked bread filled his home again.

Just as there is a second set of tablets, there are second loaves of challa. God gave woman the gift of preparation and reparation. During the Ten Days of Repentance we pray to God to gather us back. We ask God to gather in all those who were battered and to add them to the batter. Let us succeed in kneading them so that they grow to need us. Let them be light and sweet, full of air and spirit. May we be able to say with the psalmist, "I was young and now I am old, and I have never seen the righteous forsaken or their children begging for bread" (Ps. 37:25).

With Our Tears

The kabbalists regard a woman's tears as a uniquely feminine strength that bears a special relationship to the period leading up to Yom Kippur. The Talmud teaches that women cry readily (Bava Metzia 59a). According to the Ari (Rabbi Yitzchak Luria, 1534–1572), there is a special gate known as the gate of tears, and during the period of repentance, Moses himself opens this gate for anyone who is weeping. Recall that when Moses was saved by Pharaoh's daughter, he was crying: "She opened it and saw the child, and behold the boy was crying" (Ex. 2:6). In just another moment he would have drowned in the waters of the Nile on account of Pharaoh's evil decree, as did many other babies like him.

His tears saved him because they elicited the compassion of Pharaoh's daughter, who drew him out.

At this time of year there is another way in. At the entrance stands Moses, the first leader of the Jewish nation, who is also the first one to cry. He carries our tears through the gate of tears, and he is there to unleash the floodgates of divine compassion on our behalf.

God first asks of us, "Show Me your face." Then God requests, "Let Me hear your voice" (Song of Songs 2:14). Before we utter any words of prayer, our faces appear before God. Rabbi Ben-Tzion Mutzafi, a contemporary Sephardic rabbi in Israel, writes that every person is born with the image of God imprinted on his face. But over the course of our lives, our sins distort our countenance and wipe out the image of God.

For most of us, our faces have become marred by sin. But the tears that flow down our faces can cleanse and burnish the image of God. In the stirring liturgical poem recited at the beginning of Yom Kippur, "My Longing, My God, Is for You," we say: "I pour out my tears to You / Wipe away my sins as I cry." Rabbi Eliyahu de Vidas (1518–1587), author of *Reshit Chokhma*, writes that this is the source of the custom of washing one's forehead with one's tears in order to erase the sins inscribed on it.[1]

This cleansing removes the masks that cover our faces and restores the splendor of youth to our skin.

---

1   *Reshit Chokhma*, "Gateway of Repentance," 5.

Everything Can Be Overturned

For on this day atonement shall be made for you to cleanse you of all your sins; you shall be clean before the Lord.

Lev. 16:30

"On this day" – everything can happen. Everything can be overturned.

It seems inconceivable that tensions that have been simmering for years can dissipate in a single moment of reconciliation. It seems impossible that suddenly one day we could turn over a new leaf and start afresh.

Jonah the prophet cannot handle the notion of sudden

reversal. Can the great Assyrian metropolis of Nineveh suddenly be overturned? Can a decree of destruction suddenly be repealed? Can the people of Nineveh have a sudden change of heart and repent of their evil ways after years of sinfulness? Do such dramatic reversals really happen?

Jonah is troubled by this question. He delves deeper and deeper, trying to get to the bottom of it. Note how many times the verb "went down" appears in the book of Jonah: "He went down to Jaffa and found a ship…and went down in it to sail to Tarshish" (1:3–4); "And Jonah prayed…. I went down to the base of the mountains" (2:2, 5). He realizes that all his attempts to get to the bottom of things have led him nowhere. Only then does he discover the joy of sudden reversal: The fish spits him out onto dry land, the sun beats down on his head, and he is ready to die. Suddenly God creates a tree with moist, sheltering leaves, and Jonah is surprised by joy: "Jonah took great joy in the plant" (Jonah 4:6).

Immediately afterward, Jonah is in a state of distress again. A worm eats away at the plant until it is no more. Jonah is deprived of his sudden joy.

God asks Jonah, "Are you so deeply grieved?" (Jonah 4:4). God is rebuking Jonah for not believing in sudden reversals. Essentially God is saying, "You didn't believe that people could suddenly repent. But now you have seen that things can indeed be overturned instantaneously. Now you will see what it's like when everything is suddenly taken from you. One moment I gave you a plant, and the next moment I deprived you of it – because you deprived the people of Nineveh of the possibility of repentance."

Thus when Jonah recites the thirteen attributes of God, he changes the words ever so slightly. The original text reads, "A God compassionate and gracious, slow to anger, abounding in kindness and truth" (Ex. 34:6). Instead of truth, Jonah substitutes "renouncing punishment" (Jonah 4:2). In other words, Jonah has come to understand that the divine truth is the ability to forgive. God can suddenly renounce punishment, because human beings can suddenly repent. "Previously this person was detested by God, disgusting, distanced, and abominable. Now he is beloved and desirable, close and dear."[1]

---

1   Maimonides, Laws of Repentance 7:6.

Many people are prepared to repent, but they view it as a protracted process. They are unable to suddenly change their ways. They insist that they first need to examine their anger and come to terms with it. But the Rebbe of Novardok (Rabbi Yosef Yozel Horwitz, 1847–1919) teaches that the more we insist on analyzing the process, the more we distance ourselves from true repentance. The midrash relates that for 130 years, Adam pored over the question of how to repent for the sin of eating from the Tree of Knowledge. Ultimately he said just two words: "I ate – and I will continue to eat" (Genesis Rabba 19:12). Adam conceded that just as he had sinned on that one occasion, he would continue to sin in the future. There was no way around it.

The sin of the Golden Calf was a terrible betrayal that resulted in the shattering of the Ten Commandments. Moses pleaded with God, "Alas, this people is guilty of a great sin in making for themselves a god of gold. And now, if You will forgive their sin…" (Ex. 32:31–32). God responded, "I will make all My goodness pass before you" (Ex. 33:19). Immediately Moses received the gift of God's thirteen attributes of mercy, and God revealed what would happen when the people entered the Land of Israel.

Does forgiveness really take place so quickly?

Yes, and when forgiveness takes place quickly, it is all the more meaningful. When it takes a long time to forgive, everyone has already forgotten the original reason for anger, and it is only the injured party who continues to bear a grudge. But when forgiveness is immediate, as it was after the breaking of the tablets, everyone remembers both the enormity of the sin and the magnanimousness of absolution.

The new tablets were placed in the ark alongside the broken ones. Since absolution was granted so quickly, it was possible to allow space for the brokenness.

Maimonides writes, "Even though repentance and crying out to God are desirable at all times, during the ten days between Rosh HaShana and Yom Kippur they are accepted immediately."[2] The key word here is "immediately." The great joy of Yom Kippur is that everything can be suddenly and immediately overturned. Repentance can be instantaneous.

---

2 Maimonides, Laws of Repentance 2:6.

The Little Additions

Every year on Yom Kippur we plead with God, "Please do not turn us away empty-handed from before You." But what do we need to do so as not to be turned away empty-handed? Simply to live. To live fully, with energy and vitality.

In the final days and hours leading up to Yom Kippur, we need to understand that everything matters. Every little detail is significant. We cannot move through our lives like sleepwalkers. We must show God that it is worth it for Him to give us the gift of life, because we use it to the fullest. We must show God how much we enjoy our lives – this house, these children, this husband, this country. Then the angels in heaven will take note:

"Look how much energy she brings to the little things! It's worth granting her another year of life."

Our prayers, too, need to be revived. What enlivens our prayer during the ten days of repentance? Little additions, minor changes, a line here and there.

The first addition appears in the *Amida* prayer: "Remember us for life, O King who desires life, and inscribe us in the book of life – for Your sake, O God of life." The word "life" appears four times.

Then, in the second addition, we recite: "Who is like You, merciful Father, who recalls His creatures mercifully for life." The word "life" appears once again. The kabbalists explain that even as we kill our days with sin, God nonetheless grants us life. Who is like God, long-suffering.

Then we say "the holy King" instead of "the holy God." This is the most important addition to our prayers. Anyone who gets it wrong has to start over from the beginning, because this change in language encapsulates the essence of this period of repentance. We affirm that God is not just an abstract power. God is our King, who takes keen interest in us. In the words of Isaiah, "Seek the Lord where He may be found, call to him while He is close" (Is. 55:6). During the ten days of repentance, God is close. He draws close to us: "For He is coming, for He is coming to rule the earth" (Ps. 96:13). If only we realized how close He is.

The fourth addition is "the God of justice" instead of "the King who loves righteousness and justice." This is a minor emendation, but it has enormous significance. God is the embodiment of justice. We must hand God the gavel, because it is God who decides our fates now.

And finally, we say that "God makes *the* peace" instead of saying merely that "God makes peace." As noted by the Ari, the numerical equivalent of the word *hashalom*, "the peace," is the same as that of Safriel, the angel who serves as God's scribe. Each time we say this word, this angel inscribes us in the book of life. The Ten Days of Repentance include all seven days of the week. If we say *hashalom* on Tuesday, for instance, the angel writes, "May it be Your will that all of this woman's Tuesdays be wonderful." Just one letter can make all the difference.

During the Ten Days of Repentance and on Yom Kippur, we add words and letters to the prayer service that do not ordinarily appear in it so as to infuse new life into the prayers that have grown old and stale on our lips. As we recite in a liturgical poem, "Son of man, why are you sleeping? Get up and cry out to your God in supplications." Our prayer should not be tired and worn.

Rabbi Yisrael Meir Kagan (1839–1933), known as the *Chafetz Chayim*, once had a disciple who grew very ill. His colleagues did something for him which the Sages generally advise against: They donated years of their own lives to him.

"I am giving one year of my life to him," one said.

"I'm giving two," said another.

"Rabbi, how much life are you giving him?" they asked the *Chafetz Chayim*.

He thought and said, "Two minutes."

"What? That's all? But he's your beloved disciple!"

"You ought to be ashamed of yourselves," he rebuked them. "Do you not know the value of two minutes of life?"

It takes only two minutes to say these extra words in our prayers, but these additions are enormously significant.

During the Ten Days of Repentance, nothing is trivial. Every little action resounds. "Nineveh was a great city unto God" (Jonah 3:3). Everyone is great and important. A single word has tremendous value. And a single day in a single life is enormous. As Rabbi Yisrael Salanter (1809–1883) wrote:

> Ever since the destruction of the Temple, the gates of prayer have been locked.
>
> But it is well attested that there is still one prayer that is answered each and every time – and that is the prayer for divine assistance with one's spiritual life.
>
> This is the only way to pierce the impenetrable heart as with the sharp point of a needle.[1]

---

1   Rabbi Yisrael Salanter, *Or Yisrael*, 14.

What Do We Do during the Ten Days of Repentance?

Maimonides explains in his Laws of Repentance that repentance consists of three basic steps. First comes the recognition that one has sinned. A person says, "Oh no, how could I have done such a thing?" Next comes confession: "I have sinned, I have transgressed." And here it is important to note that unlike Christianity, where confession constitutes atonement, Judaism maintains that the commandment to confess is merely the beginning of a process that includes the obligation to reconcile with those we have wronged. The third step is the resolution not to repeat that particular sin in the future.

These three steps – recognition, confession, resolution – are reasonable and logical, as we would expect of Maimonides the rationalist. But then Maimonides introduces another concept that is not at all Maimonidean: remorse. Remorse is not rational but romantic. The sinner thinks, "What was I doing? What an idiot I was. And now I'm all alone."

In his book *On Repentance*, Rabbi Joseph B. Soloveitchik (1903–1993) cites the biblical story of Abigail, the wife of Nabal the Carmelite. Abigail loves her husband, a man who is landed and wealthy but also wicked. When King David arrives to kill Nabal, Abigail hastens to plead on her husband's behalf: "Do not let this be a cause of stumbling and of faltering courage to my lord that you have shed blood needlessly" (I Sam. 25:31). Her devotion is so great that she has the power to stay the arm of a king who is bent on manslaughter.

Abigail draws on the same reserves of strength to rebuke her husband for what he has done to her. Shall she be left all alone on account of his iniquity? So fervent is her devotion that her words break through to him: "His heart died within him, and he became a stone" (I Sam. 25:37). The Bible goes on to relate that "about ten days later, the Lord struck Nabal and he died" (I Sam. 25:38). In other words, Nabal the Carmelite died during the Ten Days of Repentance. This raises questions for the rabbis, because the Ten Days of Repentance are intended for those who are neither righteous nor wicked but are somewhere in the middle, whereas Nabal is clearly wicked. But his wife's devotion accrues him merit. She urges him to repent lest she be left all alone. On account of his remorse, he merits to repent.

Every one of us has an inner Abigail. In the immortal words of Rabbi Soloveitchik, "An Abigail follows every sinner."[1] When we feel most like Nabal, our inner Abigail will remind us that there is a great love that we are at the risk of losing. She will signal to us, "Repent! Turn back! Make a U-turn before it's too late." During the Ten Days of Repentance, we try to listen to this voice.

---

1   Rabbi Joseph B. Soloveitchik, _On Repentance_, ed. Pinchas Peli (Maggid Books, 2017), 11.

Yearning for Heaven

What is remorse? Rabbi Soloveitchik cites the follow-ing talmudic story:

> When Rav died, his disciples followed his casket. When they returned, they said: Let us go eat bread along the river. (Berakhot 42b)

The Talmud goes on to relate that after the disciples eat, they wonder about how they should recite the Grace after Meals. The liturgical invitation that precedes the Grace after Meals is recited only after three or more adults sit down to a formal meal. But they were in such grave distress after Rav's death that they never explic-itly stated that they were having a proper meal. The Talmud continues:

> R. Adda bar Ahava stood and reversed his cloak
> so that the tear which he had rent in mourning
> Rav was behind him. He rent another tear in his
> cloak and he said: Rav's soul has departed. And
> we have not even learned the laws of how to recite
> the Grace after Meals. (Berakhot 42b)

R. Adda bar Ahava, a man of tremendous devotion,
had already torn his cloak at Rav's funeral. In the same
way that sons tear their cloaks when their father dies,
disciples tear their cloaks when their teacher dies. But
now he turns his cloak around and makes another tear
on the other side.

"Rav's soul has departed," he says painfully. "And we have
not even learned the laws of how to recite the Grace after
Meals." He realizes that his teacher has died before he
has managed to bask in his teacher's great light.

Rabbi Soloveitchik explains why R. Adda bar Ahava is
so distressed. The disciples understand that they have
suffered a great loss. They understand that their rabbi
is no more. They have already accompanied his casket
and rent their garments. But only when confronted
with a question that they cannot answer do they

realize the enormity of their loss. Only then do they realize how much they miss their teacher on a daily basis, and how much they wish he were still with them. As Rabbi Soloveitchik writes:

> The longing for one who has died and is gone forever is worse than death. The soul is overcome and shattered by fierce longing. Just before Rosh HaShana, I imagined that my father, of blessed memory, was standing beside me. He was the one and only rebbi, master and teacher, that I ever had. I put my life down before him and said: "My father, my teacher, I have had so many new insights concerning the laws of the Day of Atonement...certainly there are amongst them some which would have pleased you, and also some which you would have rejected...." That was how I imagined myself speaking to my father, knowing that I would receive no response. O, what would I have given to be able to discuss Torah with him, if only for five minutes!...
>
> Several days ago, I once again sat down to prepare my annual discourse on the subject of repentance. I always used to discuss it with my wife, and she

would help me define and crystallize my thoughts. This year, too, I prepared the discourse, while consulting her: "Could you please advise me? Should I expand upon this idea or cut down on that idea? Should I emphasize this point or that one?"

I asked, but heard no reply. Perhaps there was a whispered response to my question, but it was swallowed up by the wind whistling through the trees and did not reach me. [1]

Rabbi Soloveitchik knows that his wife has died. Nonetheless, he reads aloud to her his insights. She of course does not respond. With each loss there is the formal mourning process, which involves understanding on an intellectual level that this particular chapter is over. But then suddenly the moment comes when the person realizes the full force of his or her grief and says, "Where am I going? What have I done, what have I lost? I'm all alone! What would I give to be back in touch with what now seems so distant."

This is the moment of the second tearing.

---

1   Rabbi Joseph B. Soloveitchik, *On Repentance*, ed. Pinchas Peli (Maggid Books, 2017), 172–173.

On Yom Kippur, we feel this sense of "what have I done." We wonder how we have gone astray and we ponder the full force of what we have lost. We realize how much we have distanced ourselves from Heaven, and how much we yearn to return to what now seems so far removed.

Rabbi Soloveitchik assures us that it is still possible. The miracle lies in repentance. We can return and reach out again:

> No matter what age he is and what stage he has reached in life, a Jew begins to long again for the Master of the Universe, in the same way as R. Adda bar Ahava longed for his master and as I long for my wife. But while our longings are a fantasy, since one who has died will never return, longing for the Master of the Universe is realistic, and man is drawn to Him and rushes toward Him with all his strength. He runs faster than he used to before he strayed afar. The intensity of the longing that bursts forth after having been pent up for so long impels him forward. For example, were I actually to see my father, would I not run after him as fast as light itself? So, too, the sinner who

has repented runs after the Creator, with all his might and strength.... This impulsion of longing raises the individual who has repented to a level above that of the thoroughly righteous man. He has not forgotten his sin – he must not forget it. Sin is the generating force, the springboard which pushes him higher and higher.... For him, the Holy One, blessed be He, does not "overlook sin" but "bears sin and iniquity."[2]

God bears sin and iniquity. He carries our sins and iniquities all the way to heaven. This is what Yom Kippur is all about. Throughout the year we say to ourselves, "Oops, I shouldn't have said that." On Rosh HaShana we tell ourselves, "We are the King's children." During the Ten Days of Repentance, we say, "I must confess what I've done." But on Yom Kippur, we tear our garments for the second time. We are overcome by yearning. We know that the heavens are within reach, but where are they?

This sense of shame, regret, and yearning will push us higher and higher until we touch the heavens once again.

---

2   Ibid., 174.

Intimate Relationships

Our intimate relationships play a key role in ensuring that we are inscribed for a good year on Yom Kippur.

Rabbi Soloveitchik writes of Abigail's tremendous feminine wisdom. As the Bible teaches, "When Abigail came home to Nabal, he was having a feast in his house, a feast fit for a king. Nabal was in a merry mood and very drunk, so she did not tell him anything at all until daybreak" (I Sam. 25:36). Abigail sees her husband drunk and reveling in his sin. And so she keeps silent. She does not say a word.

But there are times when he is sober, such as "the next morning, when the wine had gone out of Nabal"

(I Sam. 25:37). The Ten Days of Repentance are such a time. Every man, even one who seems as thoroughly wicked as Nabal, has a point at which he sobers and is receptive to rebuke. And that is when Abigail speaks up. "And his wife told him everything that had happened, and his heart died within him, and he became like a stone" (I Sam. 25:37).

Rabbi Soloveitchik writes lyrically about this moment:

> Rest assured: An Abigail watches over every sinner. Close on the trail of each sin is its punishment, its final reckoning. The sinner doesn't always give Abigail a chance to tell him the bitter truth about himself. It often happens that during the night of revelry, while the drunken party is still in full swing, Nabal is incapable of understanding what she is saying. It is even possible that, should Abigail start talking to Nabal during the wine party, she would not live to see "the morning light." However, if Abigail knows how to recognize the right moment "when the wine has gone out of Nabal" then she may say her painful words concerning "these things," and she knows how to say them, for then, as it is written, "his heart died

within him." Suddenly the sinner feels Abigail clasping his hand, and, following upon his heels, she cries out from his own heart, grips his being, giving him no peace. For her message is a terrible one, and he is utterly shaken, trembles with fear and returns to God.[1]

It is thanks to Abigail that Nabal returns to God. Thanks to the power of their intimate relationship, Nabal merits to repent before his death.

We do not always recognize the power of our intimate relationships. They are destroyed ever so quietly, in the most private chambers. People are caught up in social networks and distracted by their screens. Instead of face-to-face contact, they are connected to millions of other people who are miles and miles away. The notion of "sins between man and his fellow" was never so relevant as it is now, when so many irrelevant and insignificant connections separate us from one another, and the real connection between individuals gets sidelined. How is it possible to want just one person when there are so many people out there competing for our attention?

---

1   Rabbi Soloveitchik, *On Repentance,* 11.

This is the time to fight on behalf of intimate relationships. Cautiously, wisely. It is time to allow space for an exclusive bond: I am my beloved's. And we must do everything in our power to ensure it is reciprocated: My beloved is mine.

Part II

Praying with Transgressors

By the Merit of Transgressors

In the upper council of the heavens and in the lower council of man, we grant leave to pray with the transgressors among us.

Kol Nidrei prayer

This prayer grants unusual license. On Yom Kippur we need every good deed we can possibly summon in order to be judged favorably. Why, then, do we invite transgressors to pray among us? Shouldn't we make every effort to pray only among the righteous when we are trying so hard to avert the evil decree?

Each year during the Ten Days of Repentance, Rabbi Ovadia Yosef (1920–2013) would say, "Thanks to these transgressors, we will all merit to be judged favorably." We do not just grant license to the transgressors to pray alongside us. Rather, we entreat them to join us because we urgently need their presence.

Rabbi Yosef would relate a parable about a king who once was traveling with his son on a long journey back to the palace. When they came to the more tortuous terrain, full of muddy ditches, the king lifted his son on his shoulders. Then, when they finally arrived at the palace, they discovered that it was locked. The king turned to his son and said, "My son, I have carried you until now. Now, as we stand at the threshold, I need you to help me. The door is locked and only you can squeeze your small body through this narrow window to open the door from the inside."

After relating this parable, Rabbi Yosef would remind us that Yom Kippur is the day of small people. Only those who are "small" – only the transgressors – can cause God to open a window so that we may pass through. As the midrash on the Song of Songs teaches, "Open for me an opening like the point of a needle" (Song of Songs Rabba 5:8). In the world of strict justice where God is King, God needs the small people to squeeze through the window and unlock the door so that He can judge the world favorably. And so God pleads with us to open that door on His behalf.

Yom Kippur begins and ends with references to R. Akiva. Both in the *Kol Nidrei* prayer and in *Ne'ila*, the opening and closing prayers of Yom Kippur, we recite the verse "Light is sown for the righteous, and gladness for the upright in heart" (Ps. 97:11). During *Ne'ila* we also cry out in the *Shema* prayer: "Hear O Israel, the Lord is our God, the Lord is One" (Deut. 6:4). It was during the *Ne'ila* prayer that R. Akiva's soul departed from his body with these very words.

We encounter R. Akiva in an additional context. The Talmud (Taanit 25b) relates that once, during a long period of drought, R. Eliezer stood up and prayed, "You cause the winds to blow and the rains to fall." But his prayer was not answered. Then R. Akiva stood up and composed a prayer that was at once both old and new: "Our Father our King, hear our voices. Have mercy on us. Our Father our King, please do not turn us away empty-handed from before You." This is the first time we hear of a father who is a king, and a king who is a father.

At that point the sky became covered in clouds and the heavens opened. As the rain fell, the people whispered, "Could it be that R. Akiva is greater than the great R. Eliezer? Could it possibly be?" The Talmud responds that this is not the case. R. Akiva's prayer was answered not because he was a greater man, but because he was able to transcend petty disagreements and judge others favorably.

R. Akiva was known for his ability to look beyond the petty disagreements that drive other people apart. He had this ability on account of all that he transcended in his own life. He started out as an ignoramus who hated Torah scholars and proclaimed, "If only someone would show me a Torah scholar, and I would bite him like a donkey!" (Pesachim 49b). But then he transcended himself and became someone else entirely. And so he believes that God can transcend justice and move to a place of compassion. He has faith that the God who is responsible for drought can also be moved to bring rain.

For R. Eliezer, God is a King whose rule is one of strict justice. According to the rule of strict justice, none of us stands any chance of being judged favorably. But R. Akiva, the man who reinvented himself, knows that

God can reinvent Himself as well. God is a King, but God can also become a Father. And if God is our Father, then we are God's children, in which case the law cannot possibly be one of strict justice alone.

And so perhaps R. Akiva is truly greater than R. Eliezer. In fact just the opposite is true. R. Akiva is like the little boy whom the king asks to open the window. God accedes to R. Akiva on account of his ability to transcend himself and to transcend what would be dictated by strict justice alone.

Those who are perfect cannot conceive of a reality governed by anything other than God's rule of law. They are exacting, and they insist on the rule of truth and justice alone. But those who do not have such tremendous stature have learned how to transcend themselves. Those who have had to reinvent themselves are able to conceive of a God who can reinvent Himself as well.

If only we develop the ability to transcend the pettiness that would otherwise hold us back, we too can cause God's bounty to rain down upon us, A woman who knows how to transcend pettiness will be able to shower the world in blessing.

In words I would never dare to utter myself, Rabbi Ovadia Yosef imagines God present in the synagogue where all can see Him on a particularly difficult Yom Kippur afternoon. The situation seems hopeless. The people have transgressed, and there seems to be no chance that they can possibly be judged favorably. But then suddenly God catches sight of a transgressor in the back corner of the synagogue. He is a man who suddenly saw the light, threw on a white satin *kippa* he had once stolen from the Kotel, and showed up at synagogue at the end of the day.

"Wait a minute," God says. "What is this guy doing here? I know where he was last night. If this transgressor could transcend and transform himself so completely, then surely I can allow Myself to transcend the rule of strict justice and transform into a God of mercy." And so on account of the transgressor, God forgives the congregation.

At twenty-six points in the Yom Kippur service, we recite God's thirteen attributes of mercy, which begin as follows: "The Lord passed before him and proclaimed: The Lord! The Lord! A God compassionate and gracious" (Ex. 34:6). God passes before Moses after forgiving the transgressors who built the Golden Calf. This is a God who transcends His strict attribute of justice and transforms Himself into a God of compassion. God's tremendous compassion rains down on the world, and through the merit of the transgressors among us we are showered in blessing.

Beyond the Rule of Truth and Justice

It is a wondrous notion that people can transcend and transform themselves. It is a notion that those who hold by the strict rule of truth and justice cannot accept. Jonah the son of Amitai, whose name comes from the Hebrew word for truth, *emet*, cannot bear it. God tells him, "In forty more days, Nineveh shall be overturned" (Jonah 3:4). Jonah, the man of truth, is dismissive. He lives in a world of strict justice where such things do not happen. After all, as the Sages said, "Because the people knew that the Holy One, blessed be He, was truthful, they did not speak falsely about Him" (Yoma 69b). How can God destroy His own image?

Jonah is right, according to the rule of strict justice. A complete overturning is transgressive. It cannot be possible.

And yet it is possible, as Jonah discovers when God creates a gourd that springs up overnight and then immediately shrivels: "It appeared overnight and perished overnight" (Jonah 4:10). Jonah discovers that reality can be completely overturned. There is a divine truth that is greater than the rule of law. God "renounces punishment," as he puts it. God allows Himself to transcend the strict rule of justice because God loves His people no matter what.

Repentant sinners have tremendous faith in God's love. Those who have always been devout find such faith maddening. Perhaps God does not really love those penitents as much as they think? But for the repentant sinners, it is not all about themselves. They know full well that they are not so great. They know too that God does not love them on account of their greatness; God loves them on account of God's greatness. God loves them because God is great.

Rabbi Yitzchak ben Moshe Arama (1420–1494), author of *Akedat Yitzchak*, says that this is true faith. God is not diminished by the sins we commit because God is all-powerful. To assume that God is dependent on our behavior is heresy.

This is a tremendous revelation for those who hold by the strict rule of justice. We will not merit to be judged favorably on account of those who are perfect. According to the criterion of absolute truth, none of us would merit for God to open the gates for us. It is those who are shameful and have come from afar who truly believe that God can overturn their verdict and inscribe them in the book of righteousness. By their merit the gates will be opened.

The great truth of Yom Kippur is that atonement can happen overnight. As the Torah teaches, "For on this day atonement shall be made for you to cleanse you of all your sins; you shall be clean before the Lord" (Lev. 16:30). Maimonides writes in his Laws of Repentance, "Previously this person was detested by God, disgusting, distanced, and abominable. Now he is beloved and desirable, close and dear."[1] There is "previously" and there is "now." Today is the day to "return, O Israel,

---

1   Maimonides, Laws of Repentance 7:6.

unto the Lord your God, for you have fallen because of your sin" (Hos. 14:2).

We return to God because we have fallen and because we are sinners. And God, who is beyond the strict rule of truth and justice, opens the gate and lets us in.

Sealing Fate

> With the agreement of God and of the congregation, in the upper council of the heavens and in the lower council of man, we grant leave to pray with the transgressors among us.
>
> *Kol Nidrei* prayer

There is a heavenly council known in Hebrew as a *yeshiva shel maala*, a yeshiva in the heavenly realm. God is the head of this yeshiva, and on Yom Kippur He appoints us to serve on the admissions committee. We sit next to God behind the desk in the admissions office and we are charged to decide whether we agree to pray with each and every person who comes before us.

Why did God choose us? Because God knows that we who have known pain will not cause pain to someone else. We will insist on judging others favorably so that they do not have to suffer what we have suffered. We will plead on their behalf. No one is better suited to serve on this heavenly tribunal.

This is what happens on Yom Kippur. People who are broken and downtrodden seal the fates of others. "Tell me," God asks a woman whose daughter is ill. "What do you think; should I heal this old woman?"

Then God turns to a woman who is constantly fighting with her husband and asks, "What do you think; should I create domestic harmony for this couple?"

God waits for their response. Their word seals the fates of others. Inevitably they push God toward greater compassion. Their great love shines through. Those who have experienced pain cannot bear to cause pain to others. The woman whose son has been expelled from one school after another will not be able to expel anyone from her own school. I, who have seen so many rejected boys loitering in downtown Jerusalem's Zion Square, opened a school for them. The name of the yeshiva means "holy stones," and the boys who come to study with us come from dark streets and back alleys. I do not say no to a single mother. I do not turn away a single child. All are precious stones. The only admission criterion in our school is the desire to enter. "My longing, my God, is for You."

Yom Kippur begins when a person comes before God with a request to be accepted to the heavenly yeshiva. Does she have a letter of recommendation?

"No," she says. "I'm not such a great person."

Does she have a transcript?

"Actually I don't," she says, feeling a little embarrassed.

So what did she bring?

"I brought my good eye. My desire. My longing. My desire and love is for You."

On Yom Kippur, every one of us sits beside God on the heavenly tribunal. We are unable to reject a single Jew. We cannot deny anyone happiness. We love each other too much.

We are each an emissary on behalf of the rest of the congregation. We are bound to everyone around us. The world depends on our love.

Heavenly Time

Seek out the Lord where He can be found; call to Him while He is close.

Isaiah 66:6

We have faith that we can transcend and transform ourselves because now, at this point in the year, the heavens are so close to earth. It's not that we are such angels. Rather, it's that God is such a King – a King who bends the heavens down over our heads. During this time of year, heaven and earth are so close that we are transported back to Sinai, where God spread out the firmament like a sheet over the mountain. After all, Yom Kippur is the day that Torah was given. On

Yom Kippur Moses came down from the mountain bearing the second set of tablets. Forty days earlier, on the seventeenth of the Hebrew month of Tammuz, he broke the first set of tablets when he caught sight of the Golden Calf.

The second set of tablets are not to be taken for granted. We should not take it for granted that the Holy One, blessed be He, came down to us again and bent the heavens down over us.

As Yom Kippur approaches, heaven bends toward earth yet again. It is presumably for this reason that so many people wake in the predawn hours for *Selichot* services and fast on Yom Kippur. They are compelled to respond to the call of the heavens. During this time of year we are all living on heavenly time.

This closeness demands a response from us. Seek. And you will find.

Seeking to Draw Others Close (I)

During the Ten Days of Repentance I travel around teaching in various settings, ostensibly trying to draw others close to the tradition. But in fact it is myself that I am trying to draw close. When I see tears in other people's eyes, it awakens me from my slumber.

From the first day of the Hebrew month of Elul, we sing in the *Selichot* prayers, "Son of man, why are you sleeping?" These words were not spoken by a great man, but by the boor who served as the captain of the ship that Jonah sailed on to Tarshish. His sense of common humanity would not allow him to cast Jonah into the sea. After he was forced to do so, the Sages report that all the sailors experienced a religious conversion:

> And the sailors stood and they cast away their gods. They returned to Jaffa and went up to Jerusalem and circumcised their foreskins, as it is written, "The men feared the Lord greatly. They offered a sacrifice to the Lord" (Jonah 1:16). What sacrifice did they offer? This is the blood of circumcision, which is like sacrificial blood. (*Pirkei DeRabbi Eliezer* 10)

The sailors witnessed a miracle, and it aroused them from their spiritual slumber and inspired them to repent. This is what it means to be quick to repent. The entire Jewish people, too, is quick to repent. They demand, "Prove to us that God exists." They demand instant, irrefutable evidence. "Prove to me that if I bake challa and set aside a portion of the dough, then I will be saved." This seems to be rather naive romanticism. How can repentance be so superficial? But in fact it is these people who seem so naive and superficial who will bring the rest of us back to God.

We may wonder why people return now, after a whole year spent sinning. The answer is that they return now so as to arouse the rest of us, who are sleeping.

Consider Jonah the son of Amitai, the philosopher and the man of truth. He stands before the simple sea captain and suddenly he speaks words that are so uncharacteristic: "I am a Hebrew and I fear the Lord, God of heaven" (Jonah 1:9).

In essence Jonah is speaking not to the captain, but to himself. He, the man of intellect, suddenly speaks in the language of faith because he simply cannot remain cynical when confronted by the captain's genuine faith. Inspired by the captain, he professes his own faith.

Someone who grew up in a religious home is unlikely to profess his own faith until he witnesses someone who has returned to Jewish tradition with ardent faith. I will always remember the sixteen-year-old pregnant student who sat through my seminar on Jewish values and then came up to me after a class about Shabbat observance. "Rabbanit Yemima," she said to me, "I have decided that from now on, whenever I clap hands on Shabbat, I will do so in a way that is different from the rest of the week." She had learned that this is how one ought to behave on Shabbat, and she had resolved to take this particular practice upon herself. I felt instantly humbled. I imagined that at that moment, all the angels in heaven were clapping hands for her – in a way that is different from the way they ordinarily clap, of course.

It warms my heart every time anew. My role is not to draw others close to Jewish tradition, but to let them draw me in. It is my own dormant self that I seek to awaken.

Seeking to Draw
Others Close (II)

If nothing else, in fleeing from God, Jonah the prophet safeguards the honor of the Torah.

I was once on an airplane sitting next to a man who made all sorts of assumptions. "I see you're religious. Maybe you could stop trying to make the rest of us religious. We've had enough of your religious coercion."

"Who says I want to make you religious?" I told him. "It's already too crowded over here. You're welcome to stay right where you are."

"Excuse me?" he asked, taken aback. "You're not from

one of those organizations that tries to make Jews more religious?"

"Stop thinking that Torah is trying to pursue you," I told him. "Torah pursues its own lodging," I said, quoting the Talmud (Bava Metzia 85a). "It's true that every Jew is one of God's lost possessions, and so it's a mitzva to return every Jew to God. But Torah wishes to be found wherever it is respected, and wherever it will most feel at home."

I have never been interested in making people more religious as a goal in and of itself. Anyone who feels that his soul desires Torah is warmly welcomed in my classes. But I would never try to run after anyone. Torah has tremendous value. It is wonderful to be able to draw people close to Jewish tradition, but I have no interest in running around like a peddler hawking my wares, especially if it means I'll be accused of religious coercion. That's not for me. "Happy is the one You choose and bring near to dwell in Your courts" (Ps. 65:5).

I drag myself from city to city until I nearly collapse in exhaustion. I seek out my fellow sisters. I am so proud of their love of Torah and commandments. I love all those who knock on the doors of my classes and say, "Me too, me too. I want to come in." But I am not prepared to pursue them unless they are interested in being pursued. The honor of Torah must be safeguarded.

Seeking to Draw
Others Close (III)

I understand the distress of Jonah the prophet. It makes perfect sense to me in light of my own experience.

One year, shortly before Rosh HaShana, I was in the pharmacy waiting in line to pay for my purchases. All of a sudden there was a flurry of activity and all the cashiers abandoned their posts. "It's an hour of divine favor," they explained. "We have to recite psalms along with all those Jews who are praying in Uman at the grave of Rebbe Nachman of Breslov."

I wanted to say to them, "Hold on a minute. Where did this mitzva come from? Since when do Jews who have never kept Shabbat suddenly jump up to recite psalms, leaving me all alone at the cash register?

Suddenly I understood why Jonah fled. I imagine that he was suspicious of those people who return to God only because they know that Yom Kippur is fast approaching.[1] He was fleeing from all those individuals who are quick to repent, like the sailors on board with him. The sailors watched as the storm subsided the very moment that Jonah was lowered into the sea. "Blessed be the Lord," they all proclaimed in sudden religious fervor.

Rabbi Eliyahu Eliezer Dessler (1892–1953) regards their turning to God as a lesser form of repentance, in which individuals repent out of concern and distress. For instance, when a person is concerned about a loved one who is sick, she might take it upon herself to keep Shabbat. When a person wishes to get married, she might take it upon herself not to speak negatively about other people.

Jonah looks at the people around him. He considers them to be beneath him. They are people who need to

---

1   See Rashi on Jonah 1:3.

be jolted out of their complacency in order to come to know God, and this disgusts Jonah. He disdains people who repent out of fear or distress.

Jonah has no interest in urging the people of Nineveh to repent. As he sees it, they will repent only under duress. Their repentance will be hasty but devoid of true meaning, and Jonah has no use for it. He wants to find people who return to God after deep philosophical reflection. He believes that the people of Nineveh, who would repent only out of fear, do not deserve divine forgiveness.

There is truth to Jonah's reasoning. Repentance out of love is considered to be on a much higher spiritual level than repentance out of fear. The Talmud teaches that when people repent out of fear, their intentional sins are converted to unintentional sins. But when a person repents out of love, their intentional sins are converted to meritorious deeds (Yoma 86b). Remarkably, the state of a person's sins can be completely transformed in accordance with the nature of the heart's intent.

What will happen in the World to Come? According to Jeremiah, "No longer will they need to teach one another and say to one another, 'Heed the Lord,' for all of them, from the least of them to the greatest, shall heed Me" (31:33). We will no longer need to teach ourselves to have faith, because everyone will know God. People will no longer need to hear about the terrors of the end of days in order to be jolted into repentance. God's presence will be revealed for all to see.

Until that time comes, people will engage in the lesser form of repentance. And this too is good.

Jonah, who approaches God as a man of intellect, seeks out people whose relationship with God is primarily intellectual. Even when he is swallowed up in the belly of the fish, he nonetheless composes a prayer of thanksgiving to God. He insists that true faith must come out of love. And indeed, relating to God out of love is important. We are fortunate that there are righteous people among us who remain convinced that everything is for the best and that God settles His accounts. But we also need to be human. We need to allow ourselves to feel. We need to imagine what it is like to turn to God out of a sense of need and inadequacy. We need to allow ourselves to cry out to God.

And so God puts Jonah to the test. It is quite a terrible trial. The fish spits Jonah up onto dry land, where the hot sun beats down on him and he faints. Jonah begins to cry. He wonders how long he will have to endure such pain and discomfort. God asks him, "Are you so deeply grieved?" (Jonah 4:9). Essentially God is asking him: *Are you like everyone else, who comes crying to Me as soon as things get rough for them? Is your relationship with Me also born out of need? Just you wait – your repentance, too, will eventually be of that lesser form.*

Jonah protests, insisting that the people of Nineveh are like animals who do not know their right hand from their left. God responds by rebuking him: You should be ashamed of yourself! "Should I not care about Nineveh, that great city, in which there are more than a 120,000 people who do not know their right hand from their left, and many beasts as well?" (Jonah 4:11). God tells Jonah that even beasts and even people who do not know their right hand from their left are great in His eyes.

I revel in this ending to the story. Earlier in the book, Nineveh is described as "a great city unto God"

(Jonah 3:3). In God's eyes, there are no people who are not great. No one is small in God's eyes.

Sometimes, after I have taught an inspiring class, a woman in the audience will approach me with just a tiny question. She'll say, "Rabbanit, please tell me. Will he come back to me or not?"

How can I possibly know? Am I a clairvoyant? Can I see the future? I so desperately want to envision a happy ending for this woman whose suffering makes everything seem bleak. I am not a prophet, but I know that she has profited on account of her afflictions. They have made her great.

The truth is that the vast majority of people are those who are quick to repent. According to Rabbi Dessler, this is the way that people will repent when the Messiah comes. They will repent out of sorrow and affliction, and not out of philosophical reflection. They will repent out of brokenness, fear, illness, and mighty storms at sea. In the Messianic Era, it is this lesser form of repentance that is born out of affliction that will bring about redemption. This will be the true faith, and it is desperately needed.

The real insight is that even the lesser form of repentance, born out of fear and shame, is also repentance out of love. Fear is just the trigger. When we repent out of fear, all the dormant love that is stored up inside us is awakened, and it is genuine and true, and it was there all along.

Rabbi Dessler explains that when we are so ashamed of our sins that we are inspired to repent, it is our sin that motivates us to do good. And if our sin becomes an instrument for good, then even our intentional sins become merits.

The understanding that even fear and shame can return us to God in love is what makes the people of Israel unique. "Happy are you, O Israel!" R. Akiva says in the final mishna in Yoma (8:9), the tractate that is all about Yom Kippur. "Before whom are you purified and who purifies you? Your Father in heaven."

Why does R. Akiva say "happy are you" and not "happy are we?" Why does he say "your Father" and not "our Father"? R. Akiva came to Judaism from the outside. He knows that this lesser form of repentance can awaken a yearning for the Father who is God. Ultimately it will lead to love. This lesser form of repentance will predominate because it starts with that white satin *kippa* that a Jew puts on because he wants his mother to recover from illness – but it will lead him a long way from there.

The prophet Amos teaches, "A time is coming – declares the Lord – when I will send a famine upon the land: not a hunger for bread or a thirst for water, but for hearing the words of the Lord" (Amos 8:11). When the daughters of Israel perform the commandment to set aside a portion of the challa, they are not hungry for bread. When they begin to immerse in the ritual bath, they are not thirsty for water. It begins with something that resembles hunger and thirst, but in the end it becomes something much greater – the desire to hear the words of God. We must not be dismissive of small people. There are no small people. Even Nineveh was a great city unto God.

If we can understand this, it will bring us tremendous happiness.

I've never been good at fasting. On Yom Kippur I cry out of hunger. Jonah would spit in my face if he saw how I repent. But so what? My hunger for food will lead me to a deeper hunger to hear the words of the Lord. And from there to love and faith.

Elizabeth, I Just Wanted to Tell You…

"Blessed be the name of His glorious kingdom for ever and ever!" The walls of the synagogue reverberate when we cry out these words during the *Ne'ila* service on Yom Kippur. We roar out the words that we've whispered all year long.

The kabbalists explain that the words "Blessed be the name of His glorious kingdom for ever and ever," which we recite each year upon coronating God, serve to express our wish that His kingdom should flourish for all eternity. These are words that must be spoken in a whisper, because it is not customary for a lesser person to compliment someone of much greater stature.

It would be like knocking on Queen Elizabeth's door and saying, "Elizabeth, I just wanted to tell you that I think you're the best."

But on Yom Kippur, the small people become great. "The king's glory is in a multitude of people" (Prov. 14:28). On Yom Kippur we coronate God with the words we speak, and the Divine Presence is inordinately happy.

"A parable. There was once a king's daughter who smelled the fragrant spices stuck to the bottom of the pot and craved them…. Her servants began to bring them to her surreptitiously" (Pesachim 56a). The Divine Presence is analogized to a king's daughter who craves the burnt leftovers stuck to the bottom of the pot. But it does not befit a king's daughter to scrape the bottom of the pot with a fork, so she needs to enlist the help of her servants, who sneak her the food she loves most.

On Yom Kippur we are the burnt leftovers stuck to the bottom of the pot. We coronate God aloud. "Blessed be the name of His glorious kingdom for ever and ever!" We do not just speak these words. We yell. We roar. On this one day of the year, we are not embarrassed by how small we are relative to the greatness of the Divine

Presence. On this one day of the year, the king and queen need us. They need the masses to cry out, "Blessed be the name of His glorious kingdom for ever and ever!"

Repentance of Social Protest

Jonah the prophet has no interest in exhorting the people of Nineveh to mend their ways. He is afraid of them. He worries that they will rise to power again after they have repented of their evil deeds, and then they might become an enemy of Israel.

This is essentially a political claim. Why is Jonah berated by God? Because as God knows, sometimes our indifference and alienation mask themselves as political ideology, or even pseudo-ideology. People purport to be motivated by aesthetic considerations or by a drive for social justice, when in fact they are just cutting themselves off from humanity.

This often happens with people who consider themselves ideological. They champion lofty political and social causes, but in so doing they are completely disconnected from all that is taking place on the ground. Instead of waving placards and formulating agendas, it would be better to focus on the human connection. We ought to forgive those who are closest to us for not being great. As Maimonides writes, "A person should not be cruel when forgiving."[1]

God will say to Jonah, "Look at yourself. You are so bent on social justice that you don't have even a single friend…except for the Leviathan." According to the Sages, the Leviathan is the only animal that does not have a mate. There is no female Leviathan. Rather, the Leviathan is God's companion: "You have fashioned the Leviathan to frolic with" (Ps. 104:26).

It is so important to invest in one-on-one interactions. We should not stay out late pursuing social justice while leaving our children and our spouses to fend for themselves back at home. On Yom Kippur our children should remind us of the spices stuck to the bottom of

---

1   Maimonides, Laws of Character Traits [*Hilkhot Deot*] 6:6.

the pot. They may annoy us, but they are the spice of life. We must scrape food for them from the bottom of the pot because it is they who matter most of all.

Each year we ask in the Yom Kippur liturgy: "Why have we fasted and You have not seen it? Why have we afflicted our souls, and You paid no heed?" (Is. 58:3). God, how many prayers must we recite? How much must we afflict ourselves? God, where are You?

And God responds:

> Is this the kind of fast I have chosen? A day for people to afflict themselves? Is it bowing the head like a bulrush and lying in sackcloth and ashes? Do you call that a fast, a day acceptable to the Lord? No, this is the fast I desire: To unlock fetters of wickedness and untie the cords of the yoke. To let the oppressed go free, to break off every yoke. It is to share your bread with the hungry and to take the wretched poor into your home. When you see the naked, to clothe him, and not to ignore your own kin. (Is. 58:5–7)

The fast that God desires is the fast that attunes us to the needs of those who are closest to us.

Connected to Life

On Yom Kippur we are confronted with a single question: Are we connected to life?

What is life? In Hebrew, the word for life, *chayim*, is in the plural, because the meaning of life is to be connected to God and connected to those around us. On Yom Kippur, when we are hungry and thirsty and clad in ridiculous shoes, we have only one request of God: "Remember us for life, O King who desires life, and inscribe us in the book of life – for Your sake, O God of life."

Rabbi Chaim Friedlander (1923–1986) explains that we are praying to God to remember us for life because we live on behalf of others. We ask to be remembered for life because we are oriented toward life. We are not here just for our own sakes, but to improve the lives of others.

I'm aware that this notion is not popular nowadays, when we are always being told to worry about ourselves. The philosopher Jean-Paul Sartre championed this solipsistic mentality. He famously wrote, "Hell is other people." Yet Judaism teaches not just "If I am not for myself who will be for me," but also "If I am only for myself, who am I?" Without others, our lives are meaningless. We provide for ourselves, take care of ourselves, and ensure that we stay happy and strong so that we can be the kind of people who improve the lives of others. Because life is about being connected. When we are not connected, we are no longer inhabiting the land of the living. There are no two ways about it. The opposite of connection is death.

Yes, it's exhausting. The most exhausting aspect of being human is that we always have to be connected. The Torah teaches, "With this shall Aaron enter the holy shrine" (Lev. 16:3). What is "this"? In Genesis we are told, "This one shall be called woman" (Gen. 2:23). And so "this" refers to a woman. Before the high priest enters the Holy of Holies on Yom Kippur, he has to betroth another woman, to ensure that he will be able to fulfill the commandment "to atone for himself and for his household" (Lev. 16:6). "His household" refers to his wife. If she were to die when he were in the Holy of Holies, he would not be able to fulfill this commandment (Mishna Yoma 1:1).

The high priest is connected not just to his wife and to his household. When he enters the Holy of Holies, they tie a rope around his leg in case he should die while inside and the other priests should have to drag him out. He has to remain connected to others in order to fulfill his role in the holy Temple.

Yom Kippur is all about connection. As the mishna teaches, "There were no days as joyous for the people of Israel as the fifteenth of Av and Yom Kippur" (Taanit 26b). The mishna is not talking about the ninth of Av, which is a day of mourning and sorrow, but about the fifteenth of Av, which is a day of romance, weddings, and dancing in the vineyards.

Rabbi Zvi Yehuda Kook reminds us that Yom Kippur does not atone for sins between man and his fel-

low. If we have not reconciled with others, then Yom
Kippur will not even serve to grant us atonement for
our sins against God. No matter how devoutly we
fast and pray, Yom Kippur will do nothing for us. As
Rabbi Zvi Yehuda Kook puts it, "If there are barriers
between man and his fellow, heaven forbid, there can
be no Yom Kippur. If a person holds on to his anger,
or does not attempt to reconcile with his fellow, then
why bother fasting? Yom Kippur does not exist for that
person. At all."[1]

The Torah teaches, "For on this day atonement shall be
made for you to purify you of all your sins. You shall be
purified before the Lord" (Lev. 16:30). The *Sefat Emet*
(Rabbi Yehuda Aryeh Leib Alter, 1847–1905) reads this
verse as teaching that prior to standing before God, we
must purify ourselves by reconciling with our fellow
men. Only then can we be purified before God.

Yom Kippur is essentially an enormous laundromat, or
a ritual bath. Jeremiah teaches that God is the hope of
Israel, but the Hebrew word for hope is *mekaveh*, which

---

1   Rabbi Zvi Yehuda Kook, *Sichot*, vol. 7.

is spelled the same way as the word *mikveh*, meaning ritual bath. The entire people of Israel is gathered, drained, and pooled together. We are all hoping for God.

When a person immerses in a ritual bath, there can be no barrier between the individual's body and the surrounding water. Any such barrier would prevent the individual from becoming purified. If there remain barriers between ourselves and others – if we have failed to atone for our wrongdoings – then we cannot be purified before God.

All of the Torah portions chanted on Yom Kippur relate to the issue of connection and communication. In the Torah reading on the morning of Yom Kippur, we read about the deaths of Nadav and Avihu, the sons of Aaron the priest, who die when they bring a strange fire before God. The Sages, in an attempt to explain the reason for their mysterious deaths, point to a flaw in their character – neither of them was interested in human connection. According to one explanation, they did not want to get married because they thought so highly of their illustrious lineage; with a father like Aaron and an uncle like Moses, what woman could possibly be good enough for them? According to other explanations, they did not want to have children or to be bound by Moses and Aaron's instructions.

The Torah portion read in the afternoon service is about forbidden sexual relations. These are incestuous relations that cannot lead to anything viable and lasting. They are sterile, stagnant, and stale. They are the opposite of connection.

Jonah the prophet flees from connection. When he is aboard the ship he is weighed down by the prospect of connecting with the people of Nineveh, and the ballast is so heavy that it nearly sinks the ship. He does not pray – neither for the people of Nineveh nor for his own people of Israel. He would rather die: "Lift me up and cast me into the sea," he requests (Jonah 1:12). The Sages say that anyone who could help others out but neglects to do so will end up in distress, which accounts for the reason for Jonah's sorry state.

Instead of being seen and heard, Jonah flees. He boards a ship and, during a fierce storm, he curls up in a corner and falls asleep. He is swallowed up into the belly of a fish, a mute creature like himself. Only when he ends up in the belly of a female fish, which is teeming with life, does he finally open his mouth. Amid all the little fish inside the female fish, Jonah feels connected at last.

A woman is always connected. She is always bound up in the lives of others around her. She is forever in the belly of the female fish. Every single day she lifts up her eyes to the heavens and cries out to God like Jonah.

How can we experience a divine encounter in God's holy sanctuary if we have not reconciled with others? If a woman and man are living alongside one another like strangers, without speaking to one another, they are not alive. If a woman does not speak to her mother-in-law, she is not alive. If a woman looks at her son and grits her teeth, she is as good as dead. Because life is about connection. If we are not connected, we are dead.

As Yom Kippur approaches we are flooded with remorse and recollection because we are connected to life.

Don't Be Ashamed

When the world was created, there was no shame. "And the two of them were naked, Adam and his wife, and they were not ashamed" (Gen. 2:25). The first sin committed on earth was immediately followed by a sense of shame. And so Rosh HaShana is the birthday of shame.

For us, too, shame is born on Rosh HaShana. For two days we coronate a King who will rule over us. We are God's children, and so at that moment we too become royalty. Only then are we able to say, "I have transgressed. I have betrayed. I have stolen. I have transgressed by betraying my essence as a king's daughter, and I have stolen myself away from myself. I am ashamed."

Small children do not have a sense of shame. As they get older, they begin to feel shame.

If so, then shame is a sign of self-awareness. It is a sign that we know we are the children of royalty. Psychologists would assure us that we have nothing to be ashamed of. "What's the big deal? You're just human. So what if you cried out? Get over it! Stop feeling guilty!"

But it's not enough to be human. The Torah teaches, "You should be a holy people unto Me" (Ex. 22:30). We are half human, and half holy. We are not allowed to give up on our holiness.

The first person to express this notion was Judah. When the brothers want to kill Joseph, Judah objects, "What do we gain by killing our brother and covering up his blood?" (Gen. 37:26). He says to his brothers: What would be the point of doing something that we could never stand behind? Why would we want to bear the consequences? It would be one thing to kill Joseph, if we truly felt that were the right thing to do. But to cover his blood? To cover up our actions? Where is our sense of responsibility?

Kings will come from the tribe of Judah, because he understands the meaning of royalty.

We have lost our sense of shame in the modern world, in part due to the internet. When people leave comments on the internet, they generally choose not to include their names. But we cannot send anonymous comments to God. When God inscribes our names in the book of life, He says to us, "Come sign. You are the one who did it. Sign on the dotted line." As we recite in the High Holy Day liturgy, "Each person's signature lies in it."

Our shame will remind us of our greatness. When we say, "We have transgressed," we are reminded of how far we have fallen. One who thinks he cannot be saved is essentially declaring that he is not capable of standing before God in judgment. Only the children of royalty can endure such a difficult trial. As we read in Psalms, "The Lord tries the righteous" (Ps. 11:5). Sometimes it is OK to fail. A person cannot always act righteously. But we try to act righteously enough that we can at least stand before God in judgment.

As we recite in the Yom Kippur liturgy, "To You, God, belongs righteousness, but our faces are covered in shame" (Dan. 9:7). Our shame is a virtue. Only someone who has no sense of shame will feel comfortable walking around naked. Our _ashamnu_, our admission that we have transgressed, will lead to our _bagadnu_, which comes from the Hebrew word for clothes, _beged_. Once we realize that we have sinned, we cover ourselves up. As we read in Genesis, "And God made Adam and his wife garments of skin and He clothed them" (Gen. 3:21).

The Talmud teaches that Jerusalem was destroyed because people had no shame before each other (Shabbat 119b). This is what happens when people say shameful things about one another on Facebook, or when a husband and wife fight publicly without shame. As parents, part of our job is to refuse to tolerate certain behavior. To say, "Shame on you."

The Talmud teaches that shame has great power (Gittin 119b). When read backward, the root of the Hebrew word for shame, _bosh_, is the root of the word for repentance, _shuv_. We learn from this that "one who commits a sin and is ashamed of it, all his sins are forgiven" (Berakhot 12b).

120

Rabbi Dessler explains:

> As long as a person is ashamed of sin, even just before his friend, all is not lost. Because there is something gained by deploring the sin, and this spark of truth will lead to repentance. But when a person feels no shame, not even before his friend, then the situation is one of total sin, which is a form of total spiritual annihilation, heaven forbid.

In the previous pages we have granted ourselves license to become small in stature. But we should not become too small. We have said that God needs our smallness, as it were, so that we can squeeze through the little window and open the locked door of the palace. But sometimes, instead of squeezing our way into the palace, we have remained small and helpless outside. And so with the agreement of God and the congregation, we grant leave to pray with the shameful.

Don't be ashamed to come in.

Part III

Human Relations as the Avoda Service

Until She Appeases Her Fellow

> A God compassionate and gracious, slow to anger, abounding in kindness and truth, extending kindness to the thousandth generation, bearing iniquity, transgression, and sin; cleansing.
>
> Exodus 34:6–7

Over the course of the Yom Kippur liturgy, we recite these thirteen attributes of mercy twenty-six times. The thirteenth attribute refers to God's cleansing of those who are guilty, which takes place each year on Yom Kippur.

But when we consider this verse in its biblical context, the meaning of the thirteenth attribute becomes just

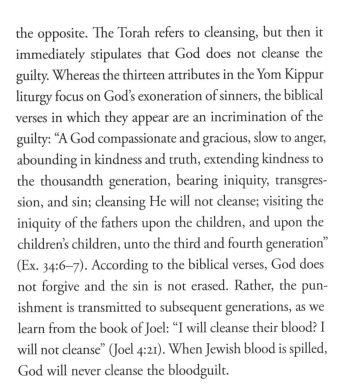

the opposite. The Torah refers to cleansing, but then it immediately stipulates that God does not cleanse the guilty. Whereas the thirteen attributes in the Yom Kippur liturgy focus on God's exoneration of sinners, the biblical verses in which they appear are an incrimination of the guilty: "A God compassionate and gracious, slow to anger, abounding in kindness and truth, extending kindness to the thousandth generation, bearing iniquity, transgression, and sin; cleansing He will not cleanse; visiting the iniquity of the fathers upon the children, and upon the children's children, unto the third and fourth generation" (Ex. 34:6–7). According to the biblical verses, God does not forgive and the sin is not erased. Rather, the punishment is transmitted to subsequent generations, as we learn from the book of Joel: "I will cleanse their blood? I will not cleanse" (Joel 4:21). When Jewish blood is spilled, God will never cleanse the bloodguilt.

So will God cleanse or not? How is it that we grant ourselves license to truncate the verse so that we come out innocent? The Sages explain that the verse refers to two different types of sins: "Cleansing" – God cleanses sins between man and God – but "He will not cleanse" sins between one person and another.

126

Imagine a dirty car that is brought in for a car wash. After it is washed and polished, it comes out looking shiny and new. Suddenly a bird swoops down and…. There goes the clean car. The front windshield is filthy again. Apparently we haven't cleaned the car after all. This is the meaning of "He will not cleanse."

As the mishna teaches, "For sins between one person and another, Yom Kippur will not atone until one person appeases the other" (Yoma 8:7).

I cannot help but wonder, if God is already wiping away our sins, why God can't also wipe away the sins between human beings and spare us the formality of apologizing to one another. It all seems to be just a show. In Hebrew, the word for apologize is in the reflexive form, like the Hebrew word for "to get dressed" or "to put on makeup," suggesting that it is all about ourselves. People walk around trying to save themselves while cheapening what it means to say "I'm sorry."

I'm sorry, but merely saying these words is not going to bring about salvation. "Cleansing – He will not cleanse!"

There is a custom of going around to all our friends and acquaintances and saying, "I ask your forgiveness.

Now please say three times that I am forgiven." The friend then replies nervously, "Forgiven, forgiven, forgiven." I experience it every year. People come up to me to ask forgiveness, but then they proceed only to dig themselves deeper.

"Rabbanit, may I ask your forgiveness?" they ask me.

"No, please, it's not necessary. I forgive you. No need to say any more."

"No, according to Jewish law, I have to tell you what I'm apologizing for. I always thought you were so superficial, and that you dress so extravagantly. Do you forgive me for having such a low opinion of you?"

"Yes."

Rabbi Jonathan Sacks notes that it is specifically those religions which focus on God's compassion and forgiveness that are responsible for so much bloodshed and cruelty throughout human history. Those who insist that their God is a God of love will most likely be confronted with a society that is less loving, because when people are convinced that all their actions are forgiven, who holds them accountable? They will feel entitled to take the law into their own hands. Far too many crusades have been embarked upon in the name of love.

By contrast, Judaism charges us with some of the responsibility for forgiveness. If others injure us, God will not erase their criminal record automatically. We have to make an effort to forgive one another. We have to weave a stronger social fabric binding us together – not in cruelty, but in compassion. Not in vengeance, but in vindication. Instead of becoming a violent society that takes the law into its own hands, God instills in us the ability to forgive. This ability ennobles us and restores us to greatness. After all, if God in all of His glory will not forgive our fellow human being unless we first forgive that person, then how can we not forgive one another? If another person will not pass through the gates of divine compassion because they have hurt us, how can we not do everything in our power to help them through? How can we not cleanse?

Just before Lighting the Candles

I create the fruit of the lips. Peace, peace, to him
that is far and to him that is near, says the Lord,
and I will heal him.

Isaiah 57:19

The fruit of our lips is peace. But it is not enough just
to have a pleasant conversation with the individual we
have wronged. According to the *Mishna Berura*, there
are certain words that need to be spoken: "I'm sorry,"
and, in response, "You are forgiven."[1]

---

1   *Mishna Berura* 606:1, 16.

"Peace, peace, to him that is far and to him that is near."
The closer we are to someone, the harder it is to make
peace. It is much easier to forgive and to reconcile with
people we do not know intimately, like colleagues at
work or a sister-in-law who lives halfway across the
country. But it's a whole other story to forgive a spouse,
or children, or the neighbors next door. If guests spill
coffee on the tablecloth, it's easy to say generously, "No
big deal; it will come out in the wash." But when it's
one of our own children who breaks a glass, it's hard
not to erupt in fury.

There was a custom among great rabbis and leaders to
reconcile with their closest family members on the eve
of Yom Kippur, just when the father or mother blesses
their children. Rabbi Mordechai Eliyahu (1929–2010)
taught that one of the moments that allows for instantaneous forgiveness occurs when a wife stands before
her husband and says to him, "I'm sorry. Now please
bless me." He then rests his hand on her head and says,
"May you have a good year." And she proceeds to say
to him, "And now you ask my forgiveness, and I will
bless you." At that point, the husband lowers his head
and the wife blesses him. Even if they were married for

decades, all their pent-up resentment dissipates in that second when the husband and wife bless one another on the eve of Yom Kippur. It's a moment of tremendous revelation.

For a husband and wife, there is so much to forgive: For her thundering silence when she is angry. For his response to her when she is angry. For his stress about household expenses. For the failure to educate the children properly at all times. For the self-righteous comments about religion, spirituality, and holiness. For the darkened face. For the degradation.

The Bible says of Samuel the prophet, "And that man came up from his city" (I Sam. 1:3). He started in his own city, and only then did he go up. To ascend the ladder of holiness we must begin at home.

Beyond Forgiveness

The Sages understood that sometimes an offense is so grievous that forgiveness seems unfathomable. The Malbim (Rabbi Meir Leibush ben Yechiel Michel Wisser, 1809–1879) went so far as to teach that forgiveness is not humanly possible:

> The definition of forgiveness is that the sin is nullified as if it never in reality existed. This is something that no human being can do, because it involves treating something that was real as if it never was. This is why, in the Bible, we never find a case where one human being forgives another. Only God forgives. [1]

---

1   Malbim on Ps. 130:4.

The Malbim contends that there is no place in the entire twenty-four books of the Bible in which one individual forgives another. Forgiveness is the province of God: "But with You there is forgiveness, so that You may be feared" (Ps. 104:4).

The Malbim is suggesting that any time we think we have truly forgiven someone who has wronged us, we are lying to ourselves, because it is impossible to pretend that something never happened. Moreover, it's impossible to forgive something truly evil. When we forgive evil, we risk becoming a part of it.

This is remarkable. As we say in the Yom Kippur liturgy, "For all these – God of forgiveness." Forgiveness is a uniquely divine capability. Even if we think we have forgiven someone, the day will come when we will find ourselves once again consumed with anger at someone who once wronged us, like the "burning coals of the broom tree" (Ps. 120:4). Such coals may be half-extinguished, but when a sudden wind blows, they are rekindled.

I once received a call from one of my students after the news was announced that a great artist had won a major prize. She told me how this artist had mistreated her many years ago. "Yemima, I can't forgive him," my student told me. "I will go to the press with it. I'll tell all. I thought I had forgiven him. I thought I had moved on, but suddenly…all my fury has been rekindled."

True forgiveness is not really emotionally possible. Even absolution is very difficult. In *El Nora Alila*, one of the liturgical poems recited in the *Ne'ila* service, we petition God to "grant us absolution," because if God doesn't grant it to us, where will we find it?

The Torah doesn't ask us to forgive or to grant absolution. We are simply asked to reconcile with one another. The Hebrew word for reconcile, *piyyus*, is an anagram of the Hebrew name for Joseph, Yosef. In essence, every Yom Kippur contains echoes of the Joseph story. For instance, during Temple times, the high priest would stand in fear and trembling before God. He would place his two hands over the head of the goat and recite his confession. The goat which the priest would lay his hands on corresponds to the goat which the brothers slaughtered after selling Joseph. It was this goat's blood that they dipped Joseph's multicolored tunic in so as to report to Jacob that their brother had been devoured by a ferocious beast (Gen. 37:33).

Moreover, on Yom Kippur we are told that the high priest would say:

> I beg of You, God, I have erred, I have been iniquitous, and I have willfully sinned before You – I and my household and the children of Aaron, Your holy people. I beg of you, God, forgive now the errors, iniquities, and willful sins that I have erred, committed in iniquity, and willfully sinned before You, I and my household.

The first word spoken by the high priest, *ana*, is an echo of the brothers' words to Joseph after Joseph revealed his identity to them: "I beg of you [*ana*], forgive your brothers the sins and wrongs they committed" (Gen. 50:17), the brothers pleaded. In response, Joseph did not declare that he had forgiven them. Rather, he said to them, "You intended to harm me, but God intended it for good, to accomplish what is now being done – the salvation of many lives" (Gen. 50:20). As Joseph tells his brothers, he arrived in Egypt for the sake of saving many lives, including theirs.

136

Joseph teaches us the meaning of true reconciliation. It is not about making our peace with evil and with evildoers, but about making our peace with what happened and where it led us. It is about being able to say to God, "Master of the Universe, from this degradation and loss of dignity, I have found salvation. I have found the energy to save many lives." It is about saying to God, "Show me Your glory" (Ex. 33:18), which is also our glory. It is about recognizing how everything that happened to us can make the world better for others, without destroying us.

My Son Joseph Still Lives

It's a struggle to reconcile ourselves with those we have wronged. And sometimes it's not just a struggle, but a full-scale military campaign. It is our own annual Yom Kippur war.

Each year, during the morning Torah reading on Yom Kippur, we read about the deaths of Aaron's sons, Nadav and Avihu. The Zohar (*Acharei Mot*) teaches that anyone who merits to weep over the death of Aaron's sons is guaranteed atonement, will be inscribed in the book of life for the coming year, and will never lose any children.

The Torah portion reads, "The Lord spoke to Moses after the death of the two sons of Aaron who died when they approached the Lord. The Lord said to Moses: Tell your brother Aaron… He is to take the two goats" (Lev. 16:1–2, 7). The mishna (Yoma 6:1) teaches that these two goats must be "identical in appearance, in height, and in monetary value, and they must be purchased together." We read further in the Torah that "Aaron is to cast lots for the two goats – one lot for the Lord and the other for the scapegoat" (Lev. 16:8).

The two goats are identical in appearance and height, and they come from the same village – so why is one of them designated as the scapegoat and sent to Azazel? Ibn Ezra, in his commentary on this verse, divides the Hebrew word into two shorter words – *ez*, meaning goat, and *azal*, meaning went. The scapegoat is the goat that went – it is the goat that becomes symbolically laden with all the sins of Israel and is then cast down a cliff until it is no more. This is the Yom Kippur war fought by all those who feel that they have been scorned and shamed and insulted. This is the struggle of all those who feel that they can barely recognize themselves anymore.

We want to live. We want to be happy again. We have so much life and vitality to share with the world.

The thirteen divine attributes refer to God as "bearing iniquity," which is about forgiveness. The ability to forgive iniquity involves bearing the inequities in life, taking them in stride, and recognizing how we who have been wronged can save others. The difficult struggles we face can enable us to help others live – as Joseph knew better than anyone else.

When two people get married, they learn to bear each other's iniquities. An iniquity is a sort of deviance, and when a man and woman get married, each deviates to some extent from the way he or she would have behaved if not for the other. No couple is perfect. Ideally a husband and wife carry one another. They learn to bear one another's deviances and to bear with one another. For instance, if the husband is a bit lazy, the wife can carry this attribute to a higher place – thanks to her husband, she can learn how to be more relaxed. If the wife is quick-tempered, the husband can learn from her how to care deeply about what matters most.

In Judaism the greatest deviance is to confuse good and evil. As Isaiah laments, "Woe to them that call evil good, and good evil; that put darkness for light, and light for darkness; that put bitter for sweet, and sweet for bitter"

(Is. 5:20). In the confessional prayer composed by Rabbi Nissim Gaon (990–1062), we beat our breasts for the sin of "permitting that which is forbidden, and forbidding that which is permitted." We are not allowed to make our peace with the existence of evil.

Rabbi Nachman of Breslov (1772–1810) writes that "when a person knows that everything that happens to him is for his own good, this perception is a foretaste of the World to Come" (*Likkutei Moharan*, Torah 4). He won't mistake the evil in another person for good. And won't look kindly upon evil. But he will learn to see everything that happens to him as having redeeming value. For instance, there are many people who will never be able to think favorably of their ex. But they can learn to look favorably on the divorce, and to be grateful for the insights that came in its wake.

Rabbi Nachman famously teaches of the importance of seeking out the good (*Likkutei Moharan* 282). He argues that the aspects of goodness we must seek out in other people and in various life situations are musical notes. Therefore the individual who leads the congregation in song and prayer on the High Holy Days must be someone who knows how to find the good in any situation.

He must be able to see the basest individual in the congregation, and to value him for the bass note he sings. Only when he stands next to the highest soprano is the prayer service beautiful and melodic. The "baseness" of one individual only serves to highlight the mellifluous heights that another can reach.

Rabbi Nachman understood that there are no bad musical notes. We can't say "So?" to the *so* or "Feh!" to the *fa*. A note is never bad; it just may sound dissonant if the notes it's combined with aren't the right ones.

The *haftara* on Rosh HaShana relates that when Hannah comes to Shiloh to pray, she mutters the prayers aloud and Eli the priest is bewildered. According to the midrash, he has to consult the priestly breastplate to interpret this woman's strange behavior. He receives a response in the form of four Hebrew letters: *kaf, shin, resh, heh.* Immediately he assumes the four letters are meant to spell *shikora*, meaning drunk. But if combined in a different order, the letters spell *keshera*, meaning kosher or fit. Hannah has to correct Eli: "No, my lord." The Sages explain that she is insisting that he is not her lord in this regard, because he has not judged her favorably (Berakhot 31b). He could have composed the notes differently. He could have read "drunk" as "fit." Essentially she tells him that he is unfit to lead the High Holy Day prayers for her, because he doesn't know the rules of composition.

When people do not know how to compose the notes properly, their prayer falls flat. When they do not know how to judge others favorably, they are unfit to serve as prayer leaders.

When my son Yosef, may he rest in peace, was still in my womb, the doctors told me that he would not live. I said that of course he would. I was sure we would prove the doctors wrong. I began referring to him as "Yosef the living." After all, in the biblical account, the brothers report that Joseph had been torn apart by a wild animal, yet ultimately his father announces, "My son Joseph still lives" (Gen. 45:28).

But to our great distress, my son Yosef did not live long. He had a heart defect and he went up to heaven in a storm at the age of fifteen months. He was so young. Every time I cry in pain for the loss of him, I hear him whispering to me from heaven not to be so sad. "And now, do not be distressed…because it was to save lives that God sent me ahead of you" (Genesis 45:5).

And it's true. That's how it was. Suddenly so many women began attending my classes. So many of them had broken hearts. My own son had had a broken heart, and so I understood where they were coming from. It was as if my son were whispering in my ear that he wanted me to learn from his broken heart how to save the lives of all those whose hearts had been broken as well.

When my son was born, I felt like such a scapegoat. Immediately after giving birth they sent me to the maternity ward to recover. I lay there and refused to allow myself to feel anything. I was surrounded by women cradling their plump new babies – each one was healthy and perfect. Only I was holding a bluish infant crisscrossed with intravenous tubes. Why was I the scapegoat?

There is no one who does not ask this question at one time or another. There is the woman who came crying to me because of the pain of being single: "Yemima," she said to me, "it's so hard. I look at this other woman. She's just like me in every way. Except that she's married, she has model children, her daughter is already pregnant – and I'm still trying to meet the right guy. My friends from school are already grandparents, and I'm still going out on dates and asking the stranger sitting across from me: 'Do you have a rabbi? Whose classes do you attend? Where do you hope to send your kids to school?' I feel like such a scapegoat."

But in the rabbinic lexicon, there is no such thing as a scapegoat. The talmudic Sages refer to the goat that was sent off the cliff not as a scapegoat, but as "the goat that is sent." It is a goat with a mission. Just as God's name is sanctified by the goat that is sacrificed, so too is God's name sanctified by the goat that is sent. Yes, it has a difficult mission, but it is a lifesaving mission. We are saved from sin on account of that goat.

This is the blessing of Joseph, who is the master of reconciliation. Even our own days of awfulness are for the sake of a greater mission – if only we can reconcile ourselves to it.

Reframing Our Narrative

The *Sefat Emet* writes that repentance on Yom Kippur is fundamentally about reconciling man to his mission. And it is no different for women.

No one says it's easy. God sends Jonah on a very difficult mission that will result in bitter exile. Jonah is charged to call the people of Nineveh to repent. If they do so, they will be deemed worthy of being exiled with the people of Israel.

"Who wants such an awful mission?" Jonah asks. "Why me?"

God tells him that it's his mission.

"But what about justice?" Jonah asks.

We do not always understand God's ways. Much is concealed, and there is much we will never know. And so we weep for the deaths of Nadav and Avihu during the Torah reading on the morning of Yom Kippur. We weep for what seems so terribly unjust. It is an incomprehensible loss.

Aaron's sons were righteous, and they died for no apparent reason. According to Rabbi Dessler, this is why the Sages offer so many possible explanations for their deaths. I want to thank Aaron for not saying, "Maybe I was a bad father. Maybe I didn't give them the best education. Maybe I'm to blame." But no. The Torah tells us that Aaron remained silent (Lev. 10:3). He understood that he was not a scapegoat – he was a messenger who was being sent on a mission much larger than himself.

Psychologists refer to this as "reframing." It is the same narrative, but we frame it differently so that it becomes something we can reconcile ourselves to. But we must proceed with humility and caution. We should never be so bold as to try to create a new frame for someone else's narrative. We are not authorized to reconcile other people with their missions. When someone encourages me to view my own situation in a different light, something inside me protests – I need to be able to create my own frame. It is tremendously liberating to be able to do so.

Rabbi Jonathan Sacks notes that many of the greatest psychoanalysts were Jews. They used the same tools as Joseph. They knew how to "bear iniquity." They knew how to take the inequities in their own lives and carry them to a new place from which they could help others. Rabbi Sacks explains that Joseph was able to reconcile with his brothers, which set a precedent for all the great psychoanalysts, most notably Victor Frankl. As Frankl writes:

> We who lived in concentration camps can remember the men who walked through the huts comforting others, giving away their last piece of bread. They may have been few in number, but they offer sufficient proof that everything can be taken from a man but one thing: the last of the human freedoms – to choose one's attitude in any given set of circumstances, to choose one's own way.[1]

---

1   Viktor E. Frankl, *Man's Search for Meaning* (New York: 1985), 86.

Viktor Frankl saved himself from physical and spiritual degradation by telling himself that he would get out of the concentration camps eventually, and then he would save others. While standing naked in the snow of the camps, he would imagine himself standing on a university stage teaching others how to deal with tragedy. By reframing his own narrative, he was able to carry himself to another place.

In one of the prayers recited in the *Selichot* service, we ask God to help us by the merit of the thirteen divine attributes of mercy. The term used for "by the merit" is *bedil,* which also means "separate." If we separate ourselves from the terrible narrative, we will be able to pass to a different place, just like God passed before Moses. We will be able to transport ourselves to a place of reconciliation and salvation.

We believe that evil will be punished. We believe that "He is a rock, His works are perfect. And all His ways are just" (Deut. 32:4). And so we must carry ourselves forward.

Even if there can be no forgiveness and no absolution, there can be reconciliation.

This does not mean we must not try to ask forgiveness; we must, and we must try to forgive. Jewish law dictates that we must. If we don't forgive others, God will not cleanse us.

But if only we could all be like Joseph. If only we could all bear iniquity and take it in stride. If only we could all carry it around with us as we set off on our mission.

The Prayer of the Abused

In the *Avoda* service, the section of the liturgy that recounts the Temple service performed on Yom Kippur, we recite the following words:

> And the priests and the people
>   standing in the courtyard –
> When they would hear the glorious,
>   awesome, ineffable name
> Emanating from the high priest's mouth,
>   in holiness and purity –
> They would kneel and prostrate themselves,
>   give thanks, fall upon their faces,
> And say: Blessed is the name of His glorious
>   kingdom for all eternity.

Rabbi Yosef Hayim of Baghdad (1835–1909), known as the *Ben Ish Chai*, offers a moving commentary on this passage.[1] He points out that the acronym of the Hebrew words for "the name of His glorious kingdom," *shem kevod malkhuto*, spell out the word Shechem, the name of the first man who dared to abuse a daughter of Israel when he raped Jacob's daughter Dinah. Anyone who abuses a woman abuses the name of God's glorious kingdom, because we women are the jewels on the divine crown.

Each year, when I encounter these words on Yom Kippur, I think of all those girls and women who have been physically or emotionally abused. Anyone who has been the victim of abuse can cry out the words, "Blessed is the name of His glorious kingdom for all eternity," drawing blessing out of a terrible curse. Such individuals can call out to God from the depths, yell at God, and cry before God, "Show me Your glory." They can restore God's lost glory, which is their own glory as well. No one need be a scapegoat. We are all

---

1 Rabbi Yosef Hayim (*Ben Ish Chai*), "Joseph Still Lives," *Parashat Vayigash*.

entrusted with a mission. From out of the disgraceful tragedies that have been committed in Israel, salvation will come to us all.

On Luck and Fate

In the beginning of the book of Leviticus, the Torah details the various activities performed by the high priest on Yom Kippur:

> And from the Israelite community he shall take two he-goats for a sin offering and a ram for a burnt offering. Aaron is to offer his own bull of sin offering to make expiation for himself and for his household. Aaron shall take the two he-goats and let them stand before the Lord at the entrance of the Tent of Meeting. And he shall place lots upon the two goats, one marked for the Lord and the other marked for Azazel. Aaron shall bring forward the goat designated by lot for the

Lord, which he is to offer as a sin offering, while the goat designated by lot for Azazel shall be left standing alive before the Lord, to make expiation with it and to send it off to the wilderness for Azazel. (Lev. 16:6–10)

Rabbi Tzvi Elimelekh Shapiro of Dinov, the *Bnei Yissaskhar*, offers a commentary on the words "Aaron shall take the two he-goats" (Lev. 16:7).[1] He explains that Aaron took the goat with words; that is, he persuaded it. The high priest spoke with the goat that was on the brink of being sent off on its mission to Azazel.

I imagine their conversation. The goat said to Aaron, "It's not fair. We two goats have to be identical in appearance, in height, and in weight. I'm exactly like the other goat. So why did God choose me to be the scapegoat? Why me?"

I can understand his question. How are we to reconcile ourselves to a difficult lot in life? To life's hardships?

The high priest would whisper in the goat's ear, "I have no idea what divine mission you are meant to carry out

---

1   Rabbi Tzvi Elimelekh of Dinov, *Bnei Yissaskhar*, Tishrei essays, 6:12.

as a scapegoat. I can't know what sort of atonement you will effect." But that was not sufficiently comforting. "You must understand," the high priest would continue. "When a person makes his peace with his lot in life, then no one will raise questions when his life takes a turn for the better. When suddenly he wins the lottery – in love, happiness, or health – no one will question whether he deserves it. Because no one asks questions about fate. Fate is beyond human control. It's a sort of supernatural power."

In the words of the *Bnei Yissaskhar*:

> "Aaron shall take the two he-goats and let them stand before the Lord" (Lev. 16:7). The Torah should have read, "And he took the he-goats." But it is similar to Elijah and the two bulls offered in sacrifice – one to God and one to Baal. They say that the bull designated for Baal did not want to go. It said, "The other bull and I grew up in the same stall. Why does he get sacrificed to God, while I get sacrificed to idolatry?" Elijah responded, "Go, because just as God's name will be sanctified by the other bull, so too will God's name be sanctified by you."

And so too with the goats on Yom Kippur. Since one goat was designated for Azazel, it might not want to be sacrificed. The high priest understands this, and so he has to win it over with words. He has to say, "There is nothing to worry about. God's commandments will be fulfilled by both of you."

This is a lesson that applies to human beings as well. Every person has to rid himself of jealousy, particularly when it comes to jealousy of someone else who is as similar to him as one goat to the other. If this lesson applies to animals, then all the more so to human beings.

No one has the right to challenge the principles and decrees of the Holy One, blessed be He. Before any decree He makes, He consults first with the heavenly hosts so that everyone will know that His rule is true and His decrees are true.

Moreover, this commandment applies specifically to the lottery. Because our lot in life is beyond our control. When the people of Israel accept whatever fate they are allotted, even when there seems to be no rhyme or reason, then it awakens the divine will. And then no one will ask any questions when God acts kindly toward them to save and redeem them – because there is no rhyme or reason when it comes to our lot in life. This serves to silence all who might otherwise wag their tongues, because there are no questions and no answers.

The *Bnei Yissaskhar* teaches how to reconcile ourselves to a difficult lot in life. We have to understand that life is a lottery. If we do not ask questions when our lot is difficult, then no one will question our good fortune when life takes a turn for the better. They will simply look at us and say, "Good for her. She deserves it."

How to Ask Forgiveness Effectively

Keep it short!

Maimonides writes in the Laws of Repentance (2:6), "Even though repentance and calling out to God are desirable at all times, during the ten days between Rosh HaShana and Yom Kippur, they are even more desirable and will be accepted immediately." During the Ten Days of Repentance, God makes it easier for us to ask forgiveness and grant absolution. Suddenly we feel a sense of reconciliation in the air.

Maimonides emphasizes that during the Ten Days of Repentance our requests for forgiveness are accepted immediately. His words are a reminder that when asking for forgiveness, we need to get right to the point. We should not waste time philosophizing or offering lengthy explanations ("I hurt you because…. I wronged you because…."). Note that in the confessional prayer, no explanations are offered. We enumerate all the ways we have sinned, but we do not explain what drove us to sin in the first place.

It's not easy to keep it short. It's so tempting to want to explain why we are right and the other side is wrong. But the proper way to ask forgiveness is simply to say, "I made a mistake," so that the other party may respond, "I forgive you." At that point, it's probably best to part ways for a while, so as not to spoil the magic of the moment.

The midrash teaches that after Adam sinned in the Garden of Eden, he fasted in repentance for 130 years. Ultimately he concluded that not only did he eat from the Tree of Knowledge, but he would continue to do so. It took him 130 years to arrive at this conclusion! With this long, drawn-out process, he denied himself the possibility of instantaneous repentance. Instead, he spent over a century engaged in self-examination only to then seal his fate with the declaration that he would inevitably continue to sin.

Do it kindly!

Rabbi Eliyahu Dessler offers a magic formula for asking forgiveness: "If a person is angry, he cannot grant full absolution. One should act kindly toward the person who is angry at him, because anger has its roots in taking, and it can be remedied by giving."

Why does a woman get angry at her husband? Because she was hoping for a compliment, or a show of support. Why does an employee get angry at his boss? Because he was hoping to receive a raise, or a recommendation, or just a smile of recognition.

According to Rabbi Dessler, anger is about taking, but reconciliation is about giving. The only way to move past anger is to give. If a person is angry at someone who did not give her what she hoped to receive, the best response is to shower the object of her anger with kindness. This strategy is effective because anger diminishes us. When we get angry at someone who didn't give us something we wanted, we feel needy and diminished.

By giving generously to the person who did not give to us, we restore our own sense of greatness and stature. A great person is able to forgive. Forgiveness is a sign of greatness of spirit and compassion for humanity.

Be merciful!

We must pray for the understanding that asking forgiveness is primarily something we do for ourselves: "Grant us absolution." It is something we wish to be granted for our own sakes.

The liturgy of Yom Kippur must be understood in the holy tongue. We ask God, "In anger – remember mercy" (Hab. 3:2). In the original Hebrew, the word "mercy" appears between "anger" and "remember." The role of mercy is to create distance between ourselves and our anger, so that we do not remember it so readily. Moreover, in Hebrew the word "mercy" comes from the word for womb, the place where a woman nurtures and grows life. Mercy nurtures and expands us.

The Hebrew word for absolution, *mechila*, is similar to the Hebrew word for compassion, *chemla*. On Yom

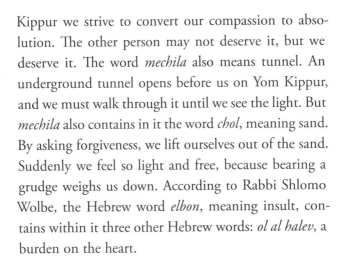

Kippur we strive to convert our compassion to absolution. The other person may not deserve it, but we deserve it. The word *mechila* also means tunnel. An underground tunnel opens before us on Yom Kippur, and we must walk through it until we see the light. But *mechila* also contains in it the word *chol*, meaning sand. By asking forgiveness, we lift ourselves out of the sand. Suddenly we feel so light and free, because bearing a grudge weighs us down. According to Rabbi Shlomo Wolbe, the Hebrew word *elbon*, meaning insult, contains within it three other Hebrew words: *ol al halev*, a burden on the heart.

When we rearrange the letters in *mechila*, we get *lechima*, which means fighting. *Lechima* sounds like *machala*, which means illness. But it can also become *machol*, dance, and *chemla*, compassion. And it can become *lechem*, bread, which nurtures and sustains. Forgiveness brings healing. Thus the prophet says, "I create the fruit of the lips. Peace, peace, to him that is far and to him that is near, says the Lord, and I will heal him" (Is. 57:19). This kind of peace and reconciliation is the forgiveness of mercy and compassion.

How Not to Ask Forgiveness

Rabbi Yisrael Salanter writes that forgiveness serves to increase peace in the world by bringing people closer to one another. It is therefore forbidden to use the act of reconciliation to hurt or distress others.

I think about all those women who came to ask my forgiveness for saying negative things about me behind my back. Give me a break. I forgive them, but I wish they hadn't bothered asking. It's also inappropriate to ask forgiveness by saying something like, "I am so sorry. For the last five years, I've found you completely unbearable. May it be God's will that I will merit to start feeling better about you." No one needs that kind of apology.

Second, it's not appropriate to say, "I'm sorry if I hurt you." It's as if one is saying, "Anyone else would not have found my actions offensive. But you're so sensitive that perhaps I offended you."

It's also rarely worth going into detail. The details are likely just to be more hurtful.

And finally, one should never say, "Fine, I'll ask your forgiveness but you need to understand that your behavior was also not OK."

The other person will understand. "They understand with their hearts and will turn and be healed" (Is. 6:10).

How Can I Help My Children Ask Forgiveness and Forgive?

First, never insist that your children ask forgiveness of one another. Forgiveness cannot be forced. Very little children cannot even understand what they are asking forgiveness for and what they did wrong.

Instead, when two children are quarreling, I bring them together and turn to one of them. "Do you forgive your sister?"

Suddenly that child feels the power of magnanimity. His honor has been restored. He concedes, 'Yes, I forgive her."

And then I turn to her. "Do you forgive your brother?"

She may refuse to play along, but that's not the end of the world. The first child has had his honor restored, and that in itself is worth something.

Sure, they will probably continue fighting. But that moment is not for naught.

165

Rabbi Avraham Yosef, the chief rabbi of Holon, relates how his parents, Rabbi Ovadia and Rabbanit Margalit, used to make amends on the eve of Yom Kippur. Rabbi Ovadia would stand there sobbing and say to his wife, "I'm sorry I did not treat you with enough respect." His wife would cry, "You? What about me? I'm sorry I didn't treat you with enough respect."

Rabbi Yosef explains that the children would cry as well. They were so moved to see their parents speak to one another that way. Immediately they would begin asking forgiveness of one another. This is a home of true greatness.

No Faking

Beware of people who only pretend to ask forgiveness. Rabbi Yeshaya ben Avraham Horowitz, known as the Shelah HaKadosh (1555–1630), writes as follows:

> If a person offends his fellow, he has to appease him. But it should not be done the way I've seen it done – where two people who get along just fine go to the study house on the eve of Yom Kippur to ask forgiveness of one another, even though they do not hate each other and have never done anything mean to one another. This is a case of truth and peace forgiving one another – even though there was no need for forgiveness in the first place. They were never at odds with one another.

The Shelah HaKadosh goes on to explain rather cynically that while friends readily rush to reconcile, enemies avoid one another. They "remain in their places in synagogue and do not approach one another, because each is waiting for the other to make the first move. And each is convinced that he is in the right and justice is on his side." He concludes, "He should hold him and not let him go! He should go to the one who is greater than him to reconcile with him, until the other responds, 'I forgive you.'"[1]

In other words, stop running to ask forgiveness from the people you like and the people who like you; they've already forgiven you, and most likely there is nothing to forgive. Instead, we must make peace with those we really don't get along with. It's easy to apologize to a close friend. The true test is to apologize to the neighbor we can't stand, and to forgive her.

---

1   _Shnei Luchot HaBrit, Rosh HaShana, Derekh Chayim_ 151.

Men and Women
Forgive Differently

According to the Sages, there is a vast difference between the way men and women forgive, and it relates back to the story of creation. Man forgives from the place where he was created, and woman forgives from the place where she was created (Nidda 31b). A woman gets offended easily, because she was created from someone else's rib. There is no such thing, for her, as a gentle ribbing. She was created from someone else's body, and so every offense is a betrayal. And it takes her a long time to forgive.

By contrast, man was created from the dust of the earth (Gen. 2:7), and he brushes off his offenses like dust. Generally speaking, it takes a lot to offend a man, and he forgives quickly. But it is hard for him to ask forgiveness of others.

When it comes to forgiveness, men are from Mars, women are from Venus. It is essential that we understand the difference.

God wants our homes to be happy, which means that our children should witness their parents forgiving one another. When conflict leads to reconciliation, children are raised in a healthy environment. Because what could be healthier than watching people mature and overcome their natural instincts? The husband, for whom apologies do not come naturally, manages to ask forgiveness nonetheless. And the wife, who is used to bearing a grudge, pushes herself to forgive him.

The mishna teaches that there are three things a man is supposed to say to his wife when night falls: "Did you tithe? Did you prepare an _eiruv_ by setting aside food? Light the candles!" (Mishna Shabbat 2:7).

Tithing is about setting aside a tenth of one's produce,

and the Hasidim associate this activity with the Ten Days of Repentance. The *eiruv* is understood to be a reference to Erev Yom Kippur, the eve of Yom Kippur. If the Ten Days of Repentance are over and Yom Kippur is about to begin but the husband and wife have still not reconciled with one another, they should embrace each other beside the lit candles.

As mentioned earlier, Rabbi Mordechai Eliyahu writes that a wife should say to her husband, "I'm sorry. Now bless me." And he should say to her, "I'm sorry. Now bless me."

The blessing over the candles creates so much light and warmth in the home, and in the world beyond.

Sacred Altercations

The Hebrew term for reconciliation, *piyyus*, is related to the word for lottery, *payis*. The mishna explains that lotteries were conducted in the Temple so as to avoid altercation and ensure peace and reconciliation:

> Initially, whoever wished to remove the ashes from the altar would remove them. And when there were many priests competing for the task, they would run and ascend the ramp [to the altar]. Any priest who preceded another and reached within four cubits of the top of the altar first was privileged to remove the ashes. And if it was a tie, the appointed priest would say to all the priests: Stick out your fingers.

And what fingers do they extend for the lottery? The first or second finger. But one does not extend a thumb in the Temple.

Once there was an incident in which both priests were tied as they were running up the ramp. One of them shoved the other and he fell and his leg was broken. And once the court saw that things were becoming dangerous, they instituted that priests would remove ashes from the altar only by means of a lottery [*payis*]. (Yoma 22a; Mishna Yoma 2:2)

According to Rabbi Yisrael Lifschitz (1782–1860) in his commentary on the Mishna, the term for lottery is *payis* because it serves to achieve reconciliation, *piyyus*.[1] When roles are divided based on a lottery, then everyone is reconciled to his role. When a person realizes that her task is her lot in life, she becomes reconciled to it.

Why then didn't the Sages institute the lottery from the outset, prior to all the altercations in the Temple courtyard? The Talmud invokes a verse from Psalms: "In the house of God we will walk in great emotion" (Ps. 55:16).

---

1   Rabbi Yisrael Lifschitz, *Tiferet Yisrael*, Yoma 2:2.

It better befits God's glory to arrive at reconciliation after the masses have been quarreling in the courtyard. If there is a clear division of labor and everyone accepts their role unquestioningly, then there is no reconciliation; there is just indifference. God wants people to worship "in great emotion." God wants the masses to quarrel about who can get there first to clear away the ashes, because it is a sacred altercation.

God doesn't desire peace and quiet in God's sacred home, or in our homes either. God doesn't want a husband and wife to accept their own roles and never come to conflict: The wife can't just repress it all, and the husband can't just remain silent. God wants us to argue about who does what:

"I'm sorry, I'm tired. Why don't you see what's going on – you don't think they're your children too?"

"Fine, but will I ever walk into the house and see you with a smile?"

As part of the thirteen attributes of divine mercy, we refer to God as "bearing iniquity" and "cleansing." We cannot cleanse our homes until we acknowledge the filth. We must allow the altercations to happen, because they are sacred. God wants our homes to be places of great emotion, not silent monasteries. Very often, when a husband and wife argue, they are fighting over who does more of the work that needs to get done in the home, much like the priests who quarreled over who would merit to cleanse the ashen filth from the sacred altar in God's home. Moreover, a husband and wife who forgive one another are teaching their children the importance of reconciliation. They are showing their children that there can still be a second set of tablets, even after it seems like all the letters have flown into the air and will never be restored to their places.

As discussed earlier, Rabbi Ovadia Yosef would ask forgiveness from his wife Margalit before lighting the candles on Yom Kippur. He would say to her, "I'm sorry I didn't treat you with enough respect." And she would kiss him on the hand and say, "You? What about me? I'm sorry I didn't treat you with enough respect." The two of them would sob, and their children would witness this exchange and immediately begin asking forgiveness of one another.

I learned from this model that I don't need to ask my children why they are fighting. I just have to focus on my own relationship with my husband. When my husband and I are reconciled, then the children will be reconciled as well.

Every home needs emotion and excitement and an ongoing discussion about the division of responsibilities. The lotteries can be cast afterward, once the fights are over. That way everyone wins.

What is true on the domestic level is true on the national level as well. In Israel we fight about the roles we perform. One camp says, "They must go to the army!" Another counters, "No, they must study Torah." But essentially each side is arguing – passionately and emotionally – about how to contribute more fully to our national home. When each side is able to listen to the other, the house of Israel is alive and well. Only then can we bear the burden of our collective responsibilities fully, with each of us doing our part.

Flying Free

Rabban Shimon ben Gamliel says: Never were there more joyous festivals for the people of Israel than the fifteenth of Av and Yom Kippur, for on these days the maidens of Jerusalem used to go out dressed in white garments – borrowed ones, in order not to cause shame to those who did not have their own…. The maidens of Jerusalem would go out and dance in the vineyards, saying: Young men, lift up your eyes and behold whom you are about to choose for yourself; regard not beauty alone, but rather consider a virtuous family, for "Gracefulness is deceitful and beauty is vain" (Prov. 31:30). And thus it is said: "Go out, maidens of Jerusalem, and look on King Solomon, and on the crown with which his mother encircled his head on the day of his wedding, on the day of the gladness of his heart" (Song of Songs 3:11). "The day of his wedding" – this is the day of the giving of the Torah. "And the day of the gladness of his heart" – this is the day when the Temple was built, may it be rebuilt speedily in our day. Amen!

Mishna Taanit 4:8

During Temple times, at the climax of Yom Kippur, the daughters of Israel would dress in white and go out into the vineyards. They would dance and sing, "Young man, lift up your eyes!" And so the romance of the fifteenth of Av had its place on Yom Kippur as well.

The dancing, *machol*, that took place in the vineyards is also the forgiveness, *mechila*, of the daughters of Israel. A successful relationship is not about one person in the limelight, but about two people who match their steps to one another.

The *Avoda* service describes every step the high priest took in the Temple. As I read about the high priest, I find myself imagining…a woman. Like the high priest, a woman is constantly going in and out, in and out. Just as the high priest changes from white vestments to gold ones and then back to white, a woman has to change her clothes to fulfill her various roles – some official, and some less so. A woman, like the high priest, is also sometimes busy handling the livers and kidneys of dead animals. She prepares bread – like the shewbread in the Temple. She immerses in the ritual bath and then rises out and towels off, and tries never to throw in the towel.

And sometimes, like the high priest, she cries so much that people start to get suspicious – because a woman is always an object of suspicion. If she is single, people ask, "Perhaps she's too standoffish? Maybe she doesn't relate well to others? Maybe she's not warm enough?" And if she's married, she's suspected of not being a good enough mother and of not being a supportive partner to her husband.

And most of all, she doubts and questions her own worthiness.

Like the high priest in the Holy of Holies, she too has to find time to pray a short prayer. Her prayer is always short, truncated, and hasty, so that her soul will not escape her amid the pressure of all those around her. The mishna (Yoma 5:4) teaches that the high priest would pray a short prayer so as not to frighten the people of Israel. A woman also prays slowly so as not to frighten her children who need her, and so as to return to the long list of tasks that forever await her. As she prays, she hears her children clamoring for her attention.

And yes, she gets offended easily: "I'm here, in the holy sanctuary, so that you will support me. So that I'll have someone to dance with. It takes two to tango! Even God had to withdraw so that there would be a world and not a wasteland. As we learn, "He did not create it to be empty" (Is. 45:18).

But there is one thing she always forgets: How splendid was the appearance of the high priest when he exited the Holy of Holies, and how splendid she is as well. A Roman visitor offered the following description of the high priest exiting the Holy of Holies:

> When he exited, the glory was doubled. Because all the Jews who were in Jerusalem would pass before him, most of them with flaming wax

torches, and all dressed in white. All the windows were adorned with tapestries and bedecked with candles. And the priests told me that on several occasions, the priest was unable to reach his home before midnight, because of all the crowds. Even though everyone was still fasting, they would not go home until they saw if they could approach and kiss the high priest.[1]

God will reassure this woman that the work she is performing – her own *Avoda* service – is not distracting her from life. It is life itself. Because there is something that comes "before God." The Torah teaches, "For on this day atonement shall be made for you to purify you of all your sins. You shall be purified before the Lord" (Lev. 16:30). But what could possibly come "before the Lord"? The *Sefat Emet* explains that people come before God. Prior to standing before God, we must purify ourselves by reconciling with the other people in our lives. As the Talmud teaches, "Yom Kippur does not

---

1 Based on *Shevet Yehuda*, written about five hundred years ago by Rabbi Shlomo ibn Virga, who was among the Jews expelled from Spain in 1492.

atone for sins between man and his fellow until one appeases his fellow" (Yoma 85b). If a woman has taken care of the people in her life, then she has fulfilled her primary obligation.

Who lights the torches for a woman? No one. And no one dances around her. But her work is divine service nonetheless. She is forever atoning for herself and for the members of her household. She places her children in secure arks to weather the stormy waters, and she ministers to them like a Temple priest.

According to the Ari, forgiveness is about forgoing, and a woman engages in both all year long. Although she seems to be forgoing her own range of movement, she celebrates the constraint and the crowding. Husband, in-laws, one child, another child – she is always willing to crowd tighter so as to make room for others. And not only is she willing to do it, but she welcomes it.

God places tremendous value on a woman's willingness to forgo her own space and her own freedom. A woman is prepared to forgive anyone who constrains her, and this forgiveness, *mechila*, is the opposite of the dancing, *machol*, around the Golden Calf, in which the children of Israel expressed their total lack of interest in any real connection with God.

A woman's work is a corrective to Jonah's flight. Jonah runs away from God because he wants his own space: "And Jonah ran away from before the Lord and headed for Tarshish" (Jonah 1:3). He is not running away from God. He is too smart for that. Rather, he is running away from that which comes "before the Lord," namely, other people. Jonah is running away from the relationships between people, because his relationship with God is far less messy.

We often make the mistake of thinking of other people as a barrier between ourselves and the service of God. This was Adam's mistake when he said, "The woman you put here with me – she gave me some fruit from the tree, and I ate it" (Gen. 3:12). Adam thought it was good to be alone. He thought Eve was interfering with his own relationship with God by leading him astray.

But we will always have to pass through other people on our way to God, because other people stand "before the Lord." As we make our own journeys toward God, we will have to encounter other people and engage in relationships with them. Jonah wanted to disappear in the belly of the fish, and God granted his wish – but with a catch. God made it very crowded for Jonah. The belly of the whale was teeming with little fish, and it was in that very constrained space that Jonah began to pray: "In my distress I called to the Lord and he answered me. From deep in the realm of the dead I called for help" (Jonah 2:3).

This is the secret of prayer. Only when our prayers are bound up in the prayers of others will they rise to heaven. And so during the Ten Days of Repentance, people gather together to pray. Such prayer is guaranteed to be compassionate, gracious, and abounding in kindness, because we are binding our prayers to those of others, like the prayer in the Temple:

> And the priests and the people
> standing in the courtyard –
> When they would hear the glorious,
> awesome, ineffable name
> Emanating from the high priest's mouth,
> in holiness and purity –
> They would kneel and prostrate themselves,

give thanks, and fall upon their faces.
(Mishna Yoma 6:2)

These words are a climax of the prayer service on Yom Kippur morning. Upon reciting these words, all the people in synagogue fall on their faces and prostrate themselves before God. The Sages explain that a miracle occurred in Temple times: The people were able to stand tightly crowded together, and yet when they bowed they had the space they needed (Mishna Avot 5:5).

This image applies to human relationships more generally. When we are standing – when we insist on standing on our principles and not giving an inch – then things feel crowded and tight. But when we bow down and concede to others, suddenly we discover there is more space than we thought.

When we ask forgiveness, we give ourselves more space. When we air our grievances and allow others to air theirs, we discover there is more air for everyone to breathe free.

It does not come naturally, and it's no simple matter. Our relationships with others take a lot out of us. All successful partnerships and marriages, and all effective parenting, is a testament to the significant investment that nurturing these relationships demands. We have to relinquish our own space if we are to bow down and cater to the needs of others, but when we do so, we discover how expansive it feels.

According to the Ari, Jonah's name means dove, but it is also related to the Hebrew word for deceit, *ona'a*. Jonah is essentially a bird who wishes to take wing and cut through the sky. But the bird in its own flight of fancy is forever saying to itself, "If only I had the wings of a dove, that I might fly and be at rest" (Ps. 55:7).[2] The dove purports to want to fly, but it is deceiving itself, because it is essentially searching for a niche, a cranny, a mate, a dovecote, a place to rest its feet. It wants to shelter its young beneath its wings and protect them from the world's ugliness.

A woman is similar. A woman seems to crave freedom. But every woman experiences the tension between the need to take flight and the need to nest. This is the female condition. A woman wants the freedom to get

---

2   See also *Tikkunei HaZohar, Parashat Vayak'hel.*

out of the house and work for a living, but at the same time, all of her prayers are for her home, her partner, and for the protection of her young fledglings. She wants to soar, but essentially she is a homing pigeon. This is not the plight of being a woman, but the flight of being a woman. Because a woman is life, just as Eve was "the mother of all life" (Gen. 3:20). When she prays "Remember us for life," she has so much to set her sights on and to orient herself toward.

Jonah represents the need to take flight so as to make one's way home. That is how it is for women as well. They want to take flight, but they want to return home. They want to match their steps to those of another, which is the greatest dance of all.

* * *

A final word about single women: Single women fly free even as they long to do anything but. While I am so preoccupied with carving out a quiet space to pray, single women are praying fervently to have a child who might interrupt their prayer. They would be so delighted for a man to look at them concernedly from the other side of the synagogue. They can fly and dance to their heart's content, yet all they really long for is to be bound. And so as I long to fly free, I remind myself that it is my plight to be bound, and theirs to be free.

We Save the High Priest

Hasidim are known to weep during the *Avoda* service, which describes the activities of the high priest in the Temple. The pages of their prayer books are stained with tears because they are overcome by grief that we no longer have a Temple or a high priest who can offer sacrifices. There is no altar, no ark, and no ark curtain. And so what will atone for our sins?

But even the high priest was not always fit to atone for the people. The Talmud relates a story about the end of the Second Temple period, when the priesthood had become corrupt and even the office of the high priest, which was supposed to be hereditary, was bought and sold. Even though the high priest was a descendant of

Aaron, he was not worthy of atoning for the people. He was simply unable to fill his role.

One year on Yom Kippur, the high priest exited the Holy of Holies looking radiant as a king. He was accompanied by 24,000 priests dressed in white and 36,000 Levites bearing torches. But then the great Sages of the generation, Shemaya and Avtalyon, passed by, and everyone ran to kiss their hands. The high priest mocked these two Sages, who were of gentile descent: "Let the descendants of the gentile nations come in peace." They responded, "Better that we should follow in the footsteps of Aaron the priest and love peace and pursue peace, even though we are not descended from him, than that we should be corrupt like you" (Yoma 72b).

And yet we cannot help but wonder: How could a corrupt priest have exited the Holy of Holies in peace? If he was wicked, how could he possibly have atoned for the people's sins? Surely if he were unfit for the job, he would have met his death inside. He would have had to be dragged out by the rope attached to his foot.

The answer is that the high priest was not alone. As we read in the *Avoda*, the priests and the nation stood in the courtyard. The Hebrew word for courtyard, *azara*, can be vocalized differently so that it reads *ezra*, help. The high priest had assistance. He was not truly alone when he was in the Sanctuary. The people were all gathered in the courtyard, standing together as one and doing the work of reconciliation. Their presence was what assisted the high priest and enabled him to exit in peace, even if he was unworthy.

Today, when we lack a high priest, it is incumbent upon all of us to help make sure that the nation of Israel is judged favorably on Yom Kippur. We in the congregation who love peace and pursue peace have the ability to save ourselves.

This is a tremendous source of consolation. When we bow down on Yom Kippur, we are assisting the nation of Israel in court. The congregation intercedes on its own behalf – we are all prayer leaders, representing the rest of the people before God.

Part IV

With Hand on Heart

The Confessional Prayer:
Barriers Broken Down
in Darkness

Rabbi Abraham Isaac Kook (1865–1935) called his monu-
mental work on repentance *Orot HaTeshuva*, literally,
"lights of repentance." He would teach from his book
during Elul and the Ten Days of Repentance, and many
people continue to study it to this day.

But it is impossible to speak of the lights of repentance
or the light of Yom Kippur until we speak about the
darkness of sin. Reconciliation can come only after a
person first asks the questions, "What have I done?

How could I have done that? I wanted to come closer, I wanted to love more fully – how did I ruin it all?"

Rabbi Yonah of Gerona (1200–1260) writes in his book _The Gates of Repentance_, "And here are righteous people, with honest hearts. The roar of a lioness is always in their thoughts. They howl over their sins like the howl of the sea."

According to Rabbi Shlomo Wolbe, every sin is a barrier between us and the Creator. A wayward thought erects one barrier. An inappropriate word erects another. One moment of anger – yet another barrier. A thousand wayward thoughts erect a thousand barriers; a thousand inappropriate words erect a thousand more. A thousand times when we fail to live by the right values – another thousand barriers. We have erected so many barriers between ourselves and our Creator this year. How can we not regret them?

And so before the blessings that precede the _Shema_ prayer we recite a chapter of Psalms (130): "A song of ascents. From the depths I have called out to You, O Lord." With this psalm, we ask God: How have I sunk so deep? If I have sunk so deep and have fallen so far into the darkness, it is only so that I will roar out to You and ask, "What have I done? What have I done?"

This chapter of Psalms draws an explicit connection between our sins ("He will redeem Israel from all their sins") and God's protection ("I am more eager for the Lord than watchmen for the morning"). Essentially we are pleading with God not to be such a good watchman: "If you guard over all our sins, O Lord, who will withstand it?" Our sins are like enormous barriers walling us off from God. We ask God please not to keep constant watch over these barriers.[1]

How can we tear down the barriers we have erected with our sins? According to Rabbi Wolbe, the answer lies in the confessional prayer. Ten times during the Yom Kippur liturgy we recite the confessional prayer: "We have sinned, we have transgressed…." With these words we tear down the barriers between ourselves and the Master of the Universe.

The midrash on Leviticus quotes Rabbi Yitzchak, who says that the confession on Yom Kippur should be "like

---

1   See Radak on Ps. 130.

a man who fits together two boards and joins them to one another" (Vayikra Rabba 3:3). The confessional prayer is a means of joining ourselves back to God

A person is meant to be joined to the Creator. After all, we are created in the image of God. It is only our sins that separate us from God. But the moment we say, "For the sin which I have committed before You," we are once again "before God." We are once again connected.

The Torah teaches that during Temple times, one of the most important tasks of the high priest was to confess the sins of the people: "And Aaron shall lay both his hands upon the head of the live goat, and confess over him all the iniquities of the children of Israel, and all their transgressions in all their sins" (Lev. 16:21). Aaron would confess the sins of the people of Israel, and today we confess our own sins, and then repeat that confession again and again, until we have recited it ten times over the course of the day.

Rabbi Nachman of Breslov plays off the connection between the Hebrew word for confession, _vidui_, and the word for certainty, _vada'ut_.[2] He speaks of a man who

---

2   _Likkutei Moharan_, Torah 4.

becomes consumed by doubt because his sins prevent him from moving on. He is completely paralyzed. The confessional prayer serves to clear up the blockage and provide him with the certainty he needs to act.

The confessional prayer serves to clarify what is certain, and what we need to get rid of inside ourselves. It cleanses our bodies and removes all the obstructions, reminding us how essentially good we are. Thus Yom Kippur is a day of joy. The confessional prayer connects us back to ourselves, to those around us, and to God. It tears down the barriers.

We Are Not Our Sins

During the afternoon service on Yom Kippur, we proclaim that "repentance, prayer, and charity avert the evil decree." The Hebrew word for repentance, *teshuva*, comes from the same root as the word for return. Repentance is first and foremost a return to ourselves.

It starts with the recognition of how inherently good we are. Ironically, the confessional prayer – in which we say, "I have sinned, I have transgressed" – serves to remind us of our essential goodness. The very act of reciting these words is an act of repentance.

My students tell me they don't understand. They ask me, "Isn't it bad enough that I had a pretty rotten year?

Now I also have to stand up and confess how bad I am, and how much I've sinned? How can this prayer possibly help matters? And how are these prayers supposed to convince me that I'm fundamentally a good person?"

The answer is that yes, it will do us well to stand and recite this prayer. Rabbi Nachman of Breslov compares the confessional prayer to removing arrows from our flesh. The Hebrew word for confession, *vidui*, comes from the root *y-d-h*, which means hurl. Every time we say, "I have sinned, I have transgressed" and beat our chest under our hearts, we are supposed to imagine that we are removing an arrow from our bodies and hurling it far away, renouncing all connection with it. As Rabbi Nachman writes, "The ten confessions of Yom Kippur are to remove the ten kinds of arrows…. Because by means of the confessional prayer we remove the blemish of these arrows from the place they reached."[1]

As a lawyer I can attest that only those who have renounced their sins are able to confess them. If our sins are still a part of us, then we cannot bring ourselves to say, "I have sinned."

---

1   Rabbi Nachman of Breslov, *Likkutei Halakhot, Orach Chayim* 3:3.

I was once in court with a bank clerk who had stolen millions from her customers. During the summations she suddenly stood up. "I want to say something," she announced, and I saw the other lawyer's concerned look.

"Go ahead," said the judge.

"I did it," she said.

"Stop," her lawyer hushed her.

"I stole the money," she said. "And I stole not just from the customers who are listed on the indictment, but from others too."

"Your Honor, my client is not of sound mind…"

"I am perfectly sound."

The judge said to me, "See? A person who committed a sin during a moment of weakness will always confess. Because her sin is not really an inherent part of her." On the other hand, when our sin has become part of us, we can't really confess. We can't hurl it out like an arrow.

Only when we say "We have sinned" do we realize the extent to which our sin isn't actually connected to who we really are. That's why the essence of the confessional prayer is about saying just the opposite of what it seems to say, "This sin isn't really part of me. I sinned, true, but I'm not at all connected to my sin. God, it's not me. I don't understand what happened to me; it must have been just very stressful circumstances. But this is definitely not me." And with that, we renounce our sins and return to ourselves.

We All Have Sinned

Rabbi Ovadia Yosef taught that even if a woman doesn't make it to synagogue on Yom Kippur, she should still open her prayer book and recite the confessional prayer ten times: Twice in the evening, twice in the morning, twice before midday, twice in the afternoon prayer, and twice in the closing prayer of Yom Kippur.

The midrash cites a parable about a king who gives his beloved wife a necklace with ten precious stones. The wife loses the necklace and confesses to her husband, who is furious and wants to divorce her.

"But didn't my forefather Abraham endure ten trials?" she says to him. And the king forgives her.

The midrash teaches that each year, we violate all ten commandments. (Yes, even murder. All of us are guilty of violating "Do not murder" even if we've never killed anyone, because the midrash teaches that embarrassing another person is tantamount to murder.) And each year God says, "That's it. Enough. It's time to summon you for judgment."

"OK, it's true. I lost the necklace You gave me," we tell God in the confessional prayer. "But think of all the trials and tribulations I had to endure – illness, financial stress, relationship stress. Yes, I sinned, and yes, I transgressed. But I never wanted to be wicked!"

According to the midrash (*Yalkut Shimoni, Acharei Mot* 576), the ten trails that serve to defend us correspond to the ten confessions of Yom Kippur. When we say, "I have sinned, I have transgressed," it is as if we are spraying each of our sins onto God's cloak, which is white as snow. And then God's cloak is laundered.

The Maharal (Rabbi Yehuda Loew ben Betzalel, 1512–1609) explains that it is as if God is saying that our sins, *chata'im*, are God's misses, *hachtaot*. God understands that if not for the difficult circumstances we were forced to endure, we would not have sinned. If we were not poor and lonely and exiled, then surely we would not have done wrong. But God is responsible for the very circumstances that lead us to sin. God, in a sense, is like parents who are angry at a child for failing to follow in their footsteps. "You should be ashamed of yourself," the parents rebuke their son. But at night, alone in their room, they do their own accounting, asking themselves, "What did we do wrong? What didn't we give him enough of? Why is he in such distress?"

According to the Maharal, when redemption comes, Esau will be held accountable for Israel's sins, because it was Esau – the ancestor of Rome – who caused Israel to sin by imposing exile on the Jewish people. The Sages explain that the scapegoat that bears all of Israel's sins is an allusion to Esau, who is also known as Se'ir – a term that means both "hairy" and "goat." The other goat which is sacrificed is an allusion to Jacob. Esau says, "Why must I bear the sins of my brother Jacob?" But God simply takes the sins of Israel and places them on His garment. Then God launders that garment until it is white as snow, thereby removing sin from Israel, as the Maharal explains.

Rabbi Dessler notes that Yom Kippur serves to demonstrate that our sins are not stuck to us. In spite of our sins, we remain pure. Our sins are not inherent to us; they are merely a by-product of the difficult circumstances we have had to endure.

Restoring the Letters
to Their Places

"*Ashamnu, bagadnu, gazalnu,*" "We have sinned, we have transgressed, we have stolen." In Hebrew, the sins in the confessional prayer are enumerated in alphabetical order, with one sin corresponding to each letter of the alphabet. According to the kabbalists, every sin we commit erases the corresponding letter in the Torah scroll. For instance, the fact that I have stolen – *gazalti* – erases the letter *gimel* each time it appears in the Torah.

Rabbi Dessler explains that by reciting the confessional prayer, we write a new set of tablets and renew the connection between God and His people. Imagine a Torah scroll with the majority of the letters erased. Every time we say *ashamnu*, we restore the letter *alef*. Every time we say *bagadnu*, we restore the letter *bet*. With *gazalnu* we restore the letter *gimel*. Gradually all the letters in the Torah scroll are restored.

According to this notion, repentance is a form of rewriting. During the confessional prayer, we restore the lost letters. We carve out new letters and carve out a new ring, like the ring Moses carved for his wife on Sinai and gave to her saying, "Behold, you are sanctified to me in accordance with the laws of Moses and Israel."

Anyone who denies the significance of the confessional prayer is essentially denying the law of Moses and Israel, which is the law of marriage. The relationship between man and wife – like the relationship between God and Israel – allows, by its very nature, for restoration and return.

Part V

Enveloped in Mercy

Enveloped in the Thirteen Attributes of Divine Mercy

Prayer is a long channel which connects us to the Master of the Universe. But if so, why do so many of our prayers remain unanswered?

Generation after generation of rabbis have offered various answers to this question, some of which have become well-worn clichés:

> It's not that God doesn't answer, but rather that sometimes God's answer is no.

> God doesn't answer to us.

God has heard our prayer, and God will answer it at the right time.

God knows that answering our prayer now will ultimately not be for our own benefit.

Our prayer has been answered, but we just don't know it yet.

Our prayer has been answered, but for someone else's sake.

There are countless disappointing responses. At the end of the day, it is hard to find comfort when our prayers seem to fall upon deaf ears.

And then suddenly on Yom Kippur God reveals that there is one prayer that will not go unanswered: the thirteen attributes of divine mercy. The Talmud teaches that "a covenant has been made regarding the thirteen attributes that they will not return empty" (Rosh HaShana 17a). This prayer will not be returned empty to the sender; it will be filled and fulfilled.

To understand how this prayer works, we must recall that the first Yom Kippur in history fell forty days after the seventeenth of Tammuz and the sin of the Golden

Calf. No sooner than the Torah was given to Israel at Sinai, the people began dancing around the Golden Calf in a terrible act of betrayal. Forgiving them would require so much atonement, so much absolution.

Moses once again ascended Mount Sinai, where he pleaded on behalf of his people for forty days.

On the fortieth day, which was the tenth day of Tishrei, God bestowed upon Moses a tremendous gift: "God passed before him and proclaimed: A God compassionate and gracious, slow to anger, abounding in kindness and truth, extending kindness to the thousandth generation, bearing iniquity, transgression, and sin; cleansing" (Ex. 34:6–7).

These words have become pillars of the Yom Kippur liturgy. We recite them twenty-six times over the course of Yom Kippur – a number corresponding to the numerical equivalent of God's four-letter name. We say these words aloud, reminding God that He passed before Moses and allowed compassion to bypass justice. In so doing, we remind ourselves that it is possible to start over again even after a terrible rupture.

These words have tremendous power. Rabbenu Bachya (1255–1340) writes:

And you need to know
That all who understand the thirteen attributes
And know their meaning and their essence
And pray them with intention –
Their prayers will not return empty.
And behold, in our day,
    when we are in a state of exile
And we have no high priest
    to atone for our sins
And no altar to offer sacrifices upon
And no Temple
We will not be left standing before God
Devoid of our prayers
    and of the thirteen attributes.
    (Rabbenu Bachya on Ex. 34:6)

We return to that wondrous moment in which God gave Moses the thirteen attributes of divine mercy. R. Yochanan says, "Were it not explicitly written, it would be impossible to say it." The Talmud goes on to describe an image quite difficult for the human intellect to comprehend:

The Holy One, blessed be He, wrapped Himself in
    a prayer shawl like a prayer leader

And showed Moses the order of the prayer.
He said to him:
Whenever the Jewish people sin,
Let them act before Me
    in accordance with this order
And I will forgive them. (Rosh HaShana 17a)

After we sinned and transgressed with the Golden Calf, God wrapped Himself up like a prayer leader, as it were, and prayed on behalf of all of us.

This is the secret of the thirteen attributes, which will not return empty. And this is the secret of how to ensure that our prayers are accepted. If we want God to accept our prayers, we have to pray on behalf of others. As we recite in the *Selichot* service, "God, You taught us to speak thirteen attributes." God instructs us: "Let them act before Me in accordance with this order." The Hebrew word for prayer book, *siddur*, comes from the same word as "order." When we come before God with our ordered prayer book, God will forgive us.

The Thirteen Attributes as an Alternative Confession

Rabbi Ben-Tzion Mutzafi writes that the thirteen attributes of mercy are also a confession of sorts. When we recite them, we lament the fact that we are not guided by these attributes in our relationships with the other people in our lives. After all, we are commanded to walk in God's ways, and the thirteen attributes of divine mercy are some of these ways. As the midrash teaches, "Just as God is merciful – so too should you be merciful. Just as God is gracious – so too must you be gracious" (*Yalkut Shimoni, Ekev* 473). As we recite this part of the liturgy, we must think: If only I were compassionate. If only I were gracious.

"Lord, Lord, compassionate God" – If we were more compassionate, we would be better at reconciling with others. The Hebrew word for compassion, *rachamim*, comes from the word for womb, *rechem*. Compassion is the ability to grow and nurture and make space for others. If we were able to connect to those around us more expansively, everything would look different.

"And gracious" – Graciousness is the ability to stop expecting a reward for each instance of good behavior. We need to learn to give freely and to stop craving recognition.

"Slow to anger" – We mourn our anger, which destroys all the goodness inside us. Anger burns away at our relationships with others, especially with our spouse and children.

"Abounding in kindness" – This is one of the most difficult challenges in our interpersonal relationships. We cannot help but lament our own inadequacy. Yes, everyone can rally for the occasional major social justice project, especially when there is a lot of pomp and circumstance involved. But to be abounding in kindness is not about running in a marathon once a year to raise money for those with disabilities. It's about acting kindly on a regular basis – being patient with the elderly neighbor who always needs our help, smiling at the student who still doesn't understand. It's not easy. I wish that I were abounding in kindness.

"And truth" – There are so many times when we fail to act truthfully. If only I had kept my promises....

"Extending kindness to the thousandth generation" – We have a tendency to remember grievances and to bear grudges for years on end, while readily forgetting acts of kindness. By contrast, God remembers our good deeds for thousands of years.

"Bearing iniquity, transgression, and sin; cleansing" – We are not expected to say that just as God is able to overlook our wrongs and move on, so too should we overlook our grievances and move on. Rather, we are supposed to bear one another's offenses and bear with one another. We must remember that both the new tablets and the shattered tablets were placed in the ark (Berakhot 8b). There is no forgetting, but there is forgiveness. We bear our grievances and carry them with us to a place of reconciliation.[1]

---

1   Rabbi Ben-Tzion Mutzafi, _Kadosh BeTzion, Yom HaKippurim._

And so the thirteen attributes, in which we remind God how connected we are to Him, also contain a plea for a deeper connection with our fellow human beings. They reflect the notion that we can achieve connection with God only by means of our connections with other people. We must wrap ourselves up like prayer leaders and ask that we, too, be guided by the thirteen attributes of mercy. The covenant made with the thirteen attributes is that they will not return empty. When we come before God to ask to be judged mercifully, God challenges us to judge each other mercifully. God wants to see if we are able to ensure that the people around us are not left to return empty-handed.

Yom Kippur is essentially about love – the love for other people and the love for God. Each is bound up in the other. Rabbi Meir Simcha of Dvinsk (1843–1926), known as the *Meshekh Chokhma*, offers a beautiful explanation of this notion:

> The Sages taught that when one's love returns to oneself, it emerges out of opposition. For instance, the poor person loves the wealthy person because he benefits from him. And the land loves the sky because it is a source of rain. All of this love

returns to oneself. But the love that returns to the beloved emerges out of a sense of equality, resemblance, and parity, like a wise person who loves another wise person.

The _Meshekh Chokhma_ distinguishes between two types of love. There is the love that is about benefiting from others, and then there is genuine love. He asks whether our love for God must necessarily be the first kind of love, since there cannot possibly be any equality with God. How can we know that our love for God is genuine, and that it is not merely an infantile dependence? How can we know that we don't merely love ourselves and therefore love anyone who responds to our needs?

And so [this higher form of love can exist vis-à-vis God] only when an individual cleaves to God's ways and genuinely loves God. When does this happen? When he recites the thirteen attributes of divine mercy. When he says, "compassionate and gracious," he must think to himself, "Just as God is gracious, so too must you be gracious." If so, then he begins to develop a sense of identification with God, and he will cleave to God's attributes

and long for the divine. And this is genuine love.
(*Meshekh Chokhma* 18–19)

The only way to cleave to God is by cleaving to the messengers whom God dispersed throughout His world, namely, the other people in our lives. God sends us these other people – especially those who are closest to us – so that we will practice the thirteen attributes on them. When we express love for other people, we are cleaving to the divine attributes, because God loves humanity. We are making ourselves like God, who loves human beings. Just as God is compassionate, so too will we act with compassion. Just as God is abounding in kindness, so too will we perform acts of kindness. Just as God is slow to anger, so too will we try to restrain our tempers.

Only when we become similar to the object of our love can we love selflessly. Only then can we love our neighbor as ourselves (Deut. 6:5).

During the Yom Kippur prayers we recite the thirteen attributes twenty-six times. The numerical equivalent of the Hebrew word for love is thirteen. Our love for God amounts to thirteen, and God's love for us amounts to another thirteen. Together they make twenty-six, which is the perfection of the thirteen attributes. Twenty-six symbolizes this doubled, reciprocated kind of love. It is not that we love out of need. Rather, we love in much the same way as we are loved.

A misanthrope cannot love God. If we do not love other people, then our relationship with God is necessarily needy and selfish. Only when we love others can we genuinely love God, because in our love for others we become like God.

How Much Do You Weigh?

One of the thirteen attributes is "abounding in kindness." For the most part we are average human beings; very few among us are truly righteous. So, as the Talmud explains, God comes and tilts the scales in favor of kindness.[1]

But how can it be? Doesn't the Torah teach, "You shall not tilt the scales of justice" (Deut. 16:19)? How can God be abounding in kindness? That is, how can God make more of our kindness? Is this not a perversion of justice?

---

1   Rosh HaShana 17a.

The Talmud asks how exactly God tilts the scales in favor of kindness:

> How does He do this? R. Eliezer says: He pushes down on the side of the merits, as it is stated, "He will again have compassion upon us; He will subdue our iniquities" (Micah 7:19). R. Yossi bar Chanina says: He bears [i.e., raises] the side of sin, as it is stated, "He bears sin and forgives transgression" (Micah 7:18). (Rosh HaShana 17a)

Rashi explains that God pushes down the side of our merits and outweighs our transgressions. _Tosafot_ add that God "bears" iniquity, meaning that God raises the side of the scale containing our sins.

Rabbi Ezra Bick, a contemporary rabbi living in Israel, explains that every time we commit an act of kindness, God weights it more heavily than a corresponding sin, because that act of kindness has repercussions. Someone else invariably observed our behavior and was inspired to emulate it. In the thirteen attributes, this is referred to as "extending kindness." The kindness we perform extends to others, thereby making the world a better place. By acting kindly, we have sown a seed of kindness in the world, and it will multiply. And so God weights our single act of kindness more heavily.[2]

At the same time, we are told that God bears iniquity. That is, God bears the weight of our sins along with us. God is aware that we are all confronted with challenging situations beyond our control: For instance, a man may speak ill of his mother because he is living in close quarters with her, since he cannot afford to provide her with a place to live on her own. These circumstances are not entirely his fault, and so God assumes some of the responsibility for his sin.

God is abounding in kindness, and God bears iniquity. In other words, God weights our acts of kindness more heavily while also bearing the burden of our iniquity along with us.

---

2   Rabbi Ezra Bick, *In His Mercy* (Maggid Books, 2011), 50.

Part VI

Approaching Atonement

Customs and Spiritual Practices
for Erev Yom Kippur

Seven Meals for the Seven Blessings

This shall be a lasting ordinance for you: On the tenth day of the seventh month you must afflict yourselves. Do not do any work – whether the native born or the foreigner who resides among you.

Leviticus 16:29

The primary mitzva of Yom Kippur is to afflict ourselves, which the Sages understood as a set of five prohibitions: no eating and drinking, bathing, anointing, engaging in sexual relations, or wearing leather shoes. According to some opinions, only eating and drinking are biblically prohibited, whereas the other afflictions are rabbinic in origin.

On Yom Kippur we afflict our bodies, but in the twenty-four hours before the fast we are commanded to eat. The Torah teaches, "You shall afflict your souls: In the ninth day of the month in the evening, from evening to evening, you shall keep your Sabbath" (Lev. 23:32). The Sages derived from this verse that all who eat on the ninth of Tishrei – the day before Yom Kippur – are accounted as if they have afflicted themselves on both the ninth and the tenth (Berakhot 8b).

Eating on the ninth day is regarded as a major commandment which is meant to atone for all the food-related sins we committed throughout the year, such as eating non-kosher food or eating without reciting a blessing. This commandment relates back to the creation of the world, when Adam and Eve ate from the Tree of Knowledge. Their sin left a terrible moral taint, and to this day so many sins are caused by inappropriate eating and drinking. People beat themselves up for eating too much, or for acting rudely toward others merely because they haven't eaten enough.

The kabbalists teach that a person who wishes to get married should eat seven meals on Erev Yom Kippur. With each meal the person should wash hands, recite the blessing over bread, and then recite the Grace after Meals. The seven meals should be interspersed throughout the day, culminating in the final meal before the onset of the fast. The Ari explains that the first conflict between man and woman in human history took place after eating the forbidden fruit. Adam and Eve were banished from the Garden of Eden, and they divorced one another. The food we eat is a way of repairing that rupture. With each of the seven meals we eat on Erev Yom Kippur, we should think about the seven blessings recited under the wedding canopy.

One of the seven blessings reads, "Grant abundant joy to these loving companions as you gladdened your creations in the Garden of Eden of old." Just as Adam and Eve rejoiced together in the Garden of Eden before they ate from the tree, so too do we pray for God to make us (or our daughter, or our sister, or whomever we are praying for) rejoice in loving companionship in the coming year.

There can be no connection and no partnership without forgiveness and closeness, which are the focus of Yom Kippur. By forgiving and bridging distance, we can draw our beloved closer to us.

In most Jewish communities the commandment to eat on Erev Yom Kippur is focused on the final meal before the fast. Certainly there is no religious obligation to eat a full seven meals. It may sound like a rather obscure practice, but I have heard countless reports of its effectiveness. One can try it again and again from year to year. One can try it for oneself, and then, years later, for one's daughter: Seven meals for seven blessings.

Kapparot

Kapparot, the plural of *kappara*, expiation, refers to a custom that is observed in various ways. In my home we perform the custom with money (others traditionally use a live chicken) and follow the kabbalistic practice of placing eighteen coins in a bag. We use coins rather than bills because they rattle, and the noise is said to have the effect of banishing demonic forces. We wave the bag counterclockwise three times and say, "This is my replacement, this is my substitute, this is my atonement; this chicken will die and I will enter into a long and good life, and peace."

The custom of *Kapparot* is a sort of ransom that a person pays to redeem himself. At the root of this custom lies the notion that our sins cannot really be erased unless we provide some sort of compensation for the damage we have done. And so the custom of *Kapparot*, which is sometimes dismissed as primitive and antiquated, actually reflects a very enlightened conception of justice.

Setting the Table for
the Pre-Fast Meal

According to a kabbalistic tradition, the table should be set especially nicely for the pre-fast meal. The table-cloth should be white and starched. Ashkenazic Jews have the custom of lighting the candles on the table itself. Sephardic Jews fill the table with holy books and cover them with the challa cover, in the hope that the coming year will be full of spiritual sustenance and the nourishment of Torah.

Lighting Candles and Blessing Children

Yom Kippur begins with candle lighting. There is a custom to light one candle for each member of the household to ensure that they merit to lead long lives. This is known as a "candle of the healthy." If any of the candles is extinguished, it may not be rekindled on Yom Kippur, but it should be lit after the end of Yom Kippur and allowed to burn completely.

There is also a custom of lighting *yahrtzeit* candles to elevate the souls of the dead. The Sages advise not to place the *yahrtzeit* candle next to the candles lit for the living members of the household.[1]

There is a special blessing for children recited while standing beside the candles. The custom is to lay one's hands on the child's head and to recite the language of the priestly blessing (Num. 6:22–27). This is followed by the blessing for children that appears at the beginning of the *machzor* and is printed in the next chapter of this book.

But even if one does not know the traditional liturgy, it is important to bless one's children on Erev Yom Kippur. A person can just say whatever blessings come from the heart. Rabbi Alexander Ziskind, who lived in Grodno in 1818 and wrote *Yesod VeShoresh HaAvoda*, advises adding brief words of rebuke to one's blessing, such as "This year you won't fight with your sister," or "This year you will learn to control your anger." According to Rabbi Ziskind, these words of rebuke are in fact a great

---

1   See *Machzor Yesod VeShoresh HaAvoda*.

blessing that will accompany the children throughout the entire year.

There is a tradition that the moment of blessing children beside the candles corresponds to the moment when Jacob blessed his grandsons Menashe and Ephraim. Tradition holds that blessings offered at this solemn moment are fulfilled.

When my father, may his memory be for a blessing, would bless me on Erev Yom Kippur, I would break out in tears. Sometimes he would bless me in person, and sometimes over the telephone. But each time I was overcome by gratitude that my father was still present to bless me, and that I merited his blessing.

Rabbi Eliezer Papo (1785–1826), known as the *Pele Yoetz*, writes that blessing children at the start of Yom Kippur serves to counteract any curses that might otherwise threaten them. The blessing offered by a mother or father, even if offered over the telephone, serves to ward off any evil decree that looms. This moment of blessing children is one of tremendous divine mercy, in which the parents are able to tear open the fabric of the heavens for the sake of their children. It is hard for the parents not to cry.

The blessing of one's children is a magical moment that takes place just prior to leaving for synagogue for the *Kol Nidrei* prayer. It is a very stressful time, but it is important not to miss this opportunity. As every mother and father knows, sometimes the only way we can help our children is by tearing open the fabric of the heavens.

The Blessing for Children on Erev Yom Kippur

For a son:	For a daughter:
May God make you like Ephraim and Menashe.	May God make you like Sarah, Rebecca, Rachel, and Leah.

May the Lord bless and protect you.
May the Lord make His face shine on you and be
gracious to you.
May the Lord turn His face toward you and grant
you peace.

May it be the will of our Father in heaven
That He place the love and awe of Him
into your heart
And that the awe of the Lord be with you
throughout your days,
That you do not sin.
That your ardor be all for the Torah
and the commandments.
That your eyes gaze straight before you,
Your mouth speak wisdom
And your heart ponder what it holds in awe.
May your hands be busy with the commandments,

And your legs run to do the will
of your Father in heaven.
And may He grant you sons and daughters,
each one righteous
And engaged with the Torah and
commandments all their days,
And may your wellspring be blessed.
May God bring you your sustenance in lawful ways,
Coming easily and liberally and from His broad hand,
And not from the hands of human beings,
So that you may be free to serve the Lord.
And may you be written and sealed
for a good, long life,
Together with all the righteous of Israel. Amen.[2]

---

2   Translation from the Koren Sacks Yom Kippur *machzor.*

Part VII

*When Entering and
Exiting the Holy*

The Kol Nidrei Prayer

With the agreement of the Omnipresent,
And of the community,
In the upper council of heaven,
And in the lower council of man,
We give leave to pray
With the transgressors among us.

Three times:
Every vow and bind, oath, ban, restriction, penalty,
And every term that sets things out of bounds
All that we vow or swear, ban, or bar from ourselves
From last Yom Kippur to this,
And from this Yom Kippur until that which is to come –

Let it be for good –
Each one, we regret.
Let each be released,
Forgotten, halted, null and void,
Without power and without hold.
What we vow is not vowed,
What we bind is not bound,
And what we swear is not sworn.

Three times:
And all the congregation of Israel are forgiven,
Along with the strangers living in their midst;
For they acted without knowing what they did.

Please forgive this people's iniquity
In the abundance of Your kindness
As You have forgiven this people
From the time of Egypt until now,
And there it is said:
And the Lord said, I have forgiven as you asked.

Blessed are You, Lord our God, King of the Universe,
who has given us life, sustained us, and brought us to
this time.[1]

---

1   Adapted from the Koren Sacks Yom Kippur *machzor.*

Words of Joy

Over the course of Yom Kippur the high priest goes in and out, in and out of various sacred Temple chambers. There is tremendous significance accorded to all his entries and exits.

On Yom Kippur we too enter and exit. We enter into sanctity with the recitation of the *Kol Nidrei* prayer, and we exit with the recitation of *Ne'ila*.

Kol Nidrei is an emotional highpoint of the Yom Kippur liturgy. Even those who rarely set foot in a synagogue will come for *Kol Nidrei*, a prayer about the power of speech. "Every vow and bind, oath, ban, restriction, penalty…." We speak to God about all the words we uttered that bound and constrained us from the previous Yom Kippur until this one.

Words create worlds. A bad word is like a prison that holds us captive. We say so many words that create dangerous worlds which serve to bind and imprison us: "I'll never be a good mother." "This child will never learn." "Our marriage is on the rocks."

On Yom Kippur we ask to be released from the prisons we have created for ourselves. The *Kol Nidrei* prayer offers us the chance of a new beginning. We nullify these words so that they are "forgotten, halted, null and void, without power and without hold."

Is it possible to erase something out of existence? According to the Sages, a vow may be retroactively annulled only if it was based on a mistaken assumption. That is, a vow may be annulled in cases where we would not have taken the vow in the first place had we known then what we know now.

There once was a girl with an ugly, rotten tooth. A young man took one look at her and swore, "I will never marry someone so ugly." The girl's family brought her to R. Yishmael the high priest, who looked after the beauty and welfare of the daughters of Israel. He replaced the rotten tooth with a beautiful golden one. (Apparently back then, a golden tooth was considered highly attractive!)

The young man saw her and was beside himself. "I'm in love with that beautiful girl with the golden tooth!"

But how could he marry her? He swore that he never would!

R. Yishmael said to him, "When you took your vow, did you have this beautiful girl in mind?"

He said, "No," because in fact he was referring to an ugly girl at the time of his vow.

R. Yishmael permitted him to marry her. He annulled his vow because it was based on a mistaken assumption. R. Yishmael insisted that anyone who thinks that the daughters of Israel are ugly is making a grave error. And then, with great weeping, R. Yishmael spoke these immortal words: "The daughters of Israel are beautiful, but poverty tarnishes their beauty" (Mishna Nedarim 9:10).

To recite *Kol Nidrei* is ask God to understand how beautiful we truly are. All the words with which we bind

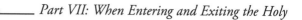

ourselves are not really us. We have simply imprisoned our beauty in verbal shackles. Our impoverished statements have tarnished us, but in essence we are all beautiful.

Our Words Are Our Bonds

I once taught a class at a women's prison in central Israel. None of the inmates really wanted to be there, but they were not given a choice. They sat there disgruntled, dressed in coarse brown uniforms. They were a diverse group – some Jewish, some Arab, and some from the former Soviet Union. What did they need to hear from me about Judgment Day when they had all been judged already? I did everything in my power to try to get their attention. I nearly gave up.

And then one of the women raised her hand. "Yes?" I asked her hopefully.

"Rabbanit, your ring – is it real?"

"Yes."

"Can I try it on?"

"Of course," I said, and I slid it off my finger, praying that I would see it again. And then, to my astonishment, my ring was passed from one woman to another, each woman trying it on her finger. Suddenly the inmates in coarse brown uniforms turned one by one into Cinderellas. These were women who had forgotten what it means to wear jewelry, to put on high heels, to get a proper haircut. Women who had preferred to forget their femininity.

I thought to myself that this was a wonderful example of a teaching from the Baal Shem Tov. I tend to think that all year long, I act like the person I really am, and then Yom Kippur rolls around and I put on a show as if I'm so pious. But in fact quite the opposite is true. All year I'm imprisoned and constrained by my own sense that I'm a sinner dressed in prison garb, and only on Yom Kippur is my true self revealed in all its goodness and purity.

On Yom Kippur I realize that all year, I've dressed myself in a coarse and ugly uniform. "He clothed himself with cursing as his garment" (Ps. 109:18). The prison uniform is like a curse – we can grow accustomed to it so easily.

I have sinned.

How have I sinned?

By betraying myself. I did not remain true to my pure essence.

During the *Kol Nidrei* prayer we shed the shackles of our own sins. And at the end of the prayer, God forgives us in accordance with His word. If we have repaired our words and our deeds, God is prepared to forgive us.

Advice for Those Who Have Trouble Fasting

The talmudic Sages teach that "it is forbidden to speak during mealtime." One should not eat and speak at the same time. But on Yom Kippur, when we are fasting, we eat our words and we are sustained by our prayers.

Rosh HaShana is a day of silence. We read about Hannah praying in Shilo: "Her lips were moving but her voice was not heard" (I Sam. 1:13). On Rosh HaShana, we stand silently amid the vast audience of onlookers as God is coronated as King. All the focus is on God. But on Yom Kippur, the focus is on human beings. As the captain of the ship says to Jonah, "How can you sleep? Get up and call out to your God" (Jonah 1:6). Yom Kippur is a day of human voices.

Communication depends on the voice: "O my dove in the cranny of the rock. Let me hear your voice" (Song of Songs 2:14).

There is a form of silent meditation known as Vipassana which is supposed to be spiritually beneficial. But when we stay silent, we are walling ourselves off from the world.

I grew up in a Lithuanian household. Our prayers were eloquent but restrained. There was no yelling or crying aloud. But Rabbi Shneur Zalman of Liadi (1745–1812), author of the *Tanya*, wrote in his will that anyone who cries out while praying will merit to have his prayers answered, because crying requires tremendous humility. And so I have learned to cry in synagogue. I have learned that God wants us to cry out from the bottom of our hearts. God wants us to yell unabashedly, "Blessed be the name of His holy kingdom forever."

The Midrash[1] contains a story about a man who used to scream out "holy, holy" whenever he recited the

---

1   *Tanna deVei Eliyahu* 13; Numbers Rabba, *Parashat Bemidbar* 4:20.

Kedusha prayer in the synagogue. When he was asked about this custom, he responded, "I am an uneducated boor. But there is one verse that I remember by heart. How can I not belt it out?" This midrash explains that God becomes great when we, in our humility, cry out His name.

According to the Ari, the Divine Presence is sustained by the food we eat all year long. Perhaps on Yom Kippur the Divine Presence is sustained by our voices instead: "Man does not live on bread alone, but on every word that comes out of the mouth of the Lord" (Deut. 8:3). When the fast is difficult and we find ourselves craving food and drink, we must remind ourselves that this is not the nourishment that will sustain us.

When we feel weakened by the fast, we should pick up the book of Psalms or leave the synagogue to speak our own words of prayer. The hunger and weakness will pass, because on Yom Kippur we are nourished by voices and sustained by prayers.

When we get hungry and tired, we tend to ask, "When will the fast be over?" But Rabbi Dessler teaches that instead we should pray, "May it be God's will that the physical afflictions that I am enduring will serve to take the place of any terrible afflictions that I would otherwise have had to endure on account of my sins." It is merely a matter of conceiving of the fast as a sort of security against an uncertain future. After all, as Rabbi Dessler explains, nothing truly takes root in our souls unless we pay for it dearly, especially with our own physical affliction.[2]

There is a story about Rabbi Yisrael Hopstein (1737–1814), the Maggid of Kozhnitz, who was very weak during the Yom Kippur fast; he went on to die twenty-four hours later. He cried out to God, "Look at me. I have arrived at synagogue so broken and shattered that I can barely speak the words of the prayers. I am drinking the minimum amount without violating the laws of the day. Why can't You speak just one line: "I have forgiven as you requested"?

All the members of the congregation then heard a heavenly voice which came forth and said, "I have forgiven as you requested."

May we all have such merit.

---

2   Rabbi Eliyahu Dessler, *Mikhtav Me'Eliyahu*, Yom Kippur 350.

God of Awe

Rabbi Avraham ibn Ezra[1]

God of awe, God of might
God of awe, God of might.
Grant us pardon in this hour
As Your gates are closed tonight.

We who have been few from yore
Raise our eyes to heaven's height
Trembling, fearful in our prayer
As Your gates are closed tonight.

---

1   Translation adapted from David de Sola Pool, 1931, https://www.
    milkenarchive.org/music/volumes/view/a-garden-eastward/work/
    american-choral-settings/.

Pouring out our soul we pray
That the sentence You will write
Shall be one of pardoned sin
As Your gates are closed tonight.

God our refuge strong and sure,
Rescue us from dreadful plight
Seal our destiny for joy
As Your gates are closed tonight.

Grant us favor, show us grace;
But of all who wrest the right
And oppress, be You the judge,
As Your gates are closed tonight.

Our forefathers' generation
Strong in faith walked in Your light
As of old renew our days,
As Your gates are closed tonight.

Gather Judah's scattered flock,
Unto Zion's rebuilt site
Bless this year with grace divine
As Your gates are closed tonight.

May we all both young and old,
Look for gladness and delight.
In the many years to come,
As Your gates are closed tonight.

Michael, prince of Israel,
Gabriel Your angels bright
With Elijah, come, redeem
As Your gates are closed tonight.

As Your Gates Are
Closed Tonight

The purpose of days – nights
The purpose of nights – Sabbaths
The purpose of the Sabbaths – the New Moon
The purpose of the New Moons – the festivals
The purpose of the festivals – Rosh HaShana
The purpose of Rosh HaShana – Yom Kippur
The purpose of Yom Kippur – repentance
The purpose of repentance – the World to Come.[1]

---

1   Rabbi Abraham Horowitz, *Brit Avraham*, 308. Also quoted in *Daf al HaDaf*, Eiruvin 65a.

We might say that the purpose of the Ten Days of Repentance is Yom Kippur, and the purpose of Yom Kippur is the *Ne'ila* prayer – because everything depends on the closing, on how we are sealed in the book of life.[2]

In other words, we come into this world for the sake of the days, and the days are for the sake of the nights, and the nights are for the sake of the Sabbaths, and the Sabbaths are for the sake of the New Moons, and the New Moons are for the sake of the festivals, and the festivals are for the sake of Rosh HaShana, and Rosh HaShana is for the sake of Yom Kippur, and Yom Kippur is for the sake of the *Ne'ila* prayer. In essence, we come into the world for the sake of *Ne'ila*. And so even if we feel weak on account of the fast, we should steel ourselves and pray with purity and clarity of thought.[3]

At the end of Yom Kippur, when it comes time for God to seal our fates, our prayers gain strength as if of their own accord. We ask God with fevered bodies but fervent hearts, "Our Father, our King, inscribe us in the book of good life." This prayer is essentially a variation

---

2   *Mishna Berura* 623:3.
3   Ibid.

on the lover's plea in the Song of Songs: "Set me as a seal upon your heart, as a seal upon your arm, for love is as fierce as death" (Song of Songs 8:6). We draw close to God as the gates are closed, and we lock ourselves in a firm embrace as they are finally locked.

Sometimes people feel like something in their life is inexplicably locked. The Sages say that this feeling can be linked to events that took place in previous incarnations, which we are unable to access. According to the midrash, this is how Elihu explained Job's suffering to him: There is law and order in creation, even if it is not always evident to us. For instance, the kabbalists teach that our whole purpose on earth may be to serve as a corrective for another person's behavior in a previous incarnation. If so, we may find ourselves locked and stymied in our efforts to achieve our goals. Nothing seems to help – not praying at the Kotel for forty days, not separating challa, not traveling to receive blessings from great rabbis.

But all is not lost. There is still that last hour before sunset as Yom Kippur wanes. Rabbi Yechiel Michel Epstein refers to this period as the time when the sun is at the tops of the trees. The Hebrew word for tree, *ilan,* contains four letters, each of which corresponds to the first letter of a word from a line in the Yom Kippur liturgy, "You extend Your hand to sinners." When the sun descends to the tops of the trees, it is as if God extends a hand from heaven and pries open the broken and rusty locks in our lives.[4]

> God of awe, God of might
> God of awe, God of might.
> Grant us pardon in this hour
> As your gates are closed tonight.

How do we pry open ancient locks? The Jerusalem Talmud (Y. Makkot 2:6) teaches as follows:

> They asked wisdom: What is the punishment for a sinner?
>
> She said to them: "Evil pursues the evil" (Prov. 13:21).
>
> They asked prophecy: What is the punishment for a sinner?
>
> She said to them: "The soul that sins shall die" (Ezek. 18:20).

---

4   *Arukh HaShulchan, Orach Chayim* 623.

They asked Torah: What is the punishment for a sinner?

She said to them: He should bring a guilt offering and it will atone for him. As it is written, "It will be accepted on your behalf to make atonement for you" (Lev. 1:4).

They asked the Holy One, blessed be He: What is the punishment for a sinner?

He said: He should repent, and this will atone for him.

How can it be that the Torah, the prophets, and the Sages offer a different answer than God? Are they not familiar with the power of repentance?

There comes a time when we have knocked on all the doors of all the great rabbis, the prophets, and the fortune-tellers, and we have discovered that they are all locked. All our knocks lead to locks. Only then do we understand that the gates on high are never locked.

When we feel weak and hungry and can't bear the fast for another moment, suddenly it is time to roar out, "Hear O Israel!" It was at this moment two thousand years ago that R. Akiva was led to his death. The Romans combed his flesh with iron combs, and as he returned his soul to his Maker, he cried out, "Hear O Israel, the Lord is our God, the Lord is One." In that moment when the sky is streaked with red and we cry out, "The Lord is One," we realize that there is One who can open up the gate that is locked inside of us.

God will see how each of us resembles R. Akiva. We too have endured tremendous suffering and pain, and we too have devoted our souls to God. _The Lord is One!_ How could God possibly doubt us? Our hearts are filled with only the One God. As the gates swing shut, we stand locked in God's embrace.

Even those who are unable to make it to synagogue for the _Ne'ila_ prayer can hear the roar that arises from all over the Land of Israel, as everyone cries out "Hear O Israel" before the sun sets. This roar bursts open the ancient locks.

And then it is time for a single tear. In that moment when the decree is sealed, we save ourselves by means of our tears. Rabbi Eliezer Papo, the _Pele Yoetz_, writes that one single tear during the _Ne'ila_ prayer can convert an evil decree into a good one. A single tear can oil the hinges of the gates that have been locked for so long. When we unleash the floodgates, we unlock the gates.

And then we touch the heavens. We cry out in a resounding roar with the entire Land of Israel, "The Lord He is God" (I Kings 18:39).

Where is the place of His glory? The Sages explain that from the first of the month of Elul until Yom Kippur, the King is in the fields. God is here, very close to us, but at the end of Yom Kippur God returns to the seventh heaven. Every time we say the words, "The Lord He is God," we accompany God back to another level of heaven. We must hold fast to the hem of God's cloak, accompanying God from one level of heaven to the next. "The Lord He is God!" By the time we recite these words for the seventh time, we are in the seventh level of heaven. According to the kabbalists, a door opens to allow for an encounter between two faces of God, the Extended Countenance and the Lesser Countenance, and between the attribute of justice and the attribute of mercy. Justice meets mercy, and mercy spills into the world. For a few moments only, every one of us resembles the high priest standing before the throne of

Part VII: When Entering and Exiting the Holy

God's glory. It is our moment to tear open the heavens. We must give voice to all our prayers!

This moment is so brief, so powerful, and so fleeting. We may feel so weak that we nearly miss it. And so we must prepare in advance.

The Talmud teaches that there are four keys that remain in God's hands and are not entrusted to any messenger: The key to marriage and childbirth, the key to livelihood, the key to rain, and the key to the revival of the dead. We are told that these matters depend not on merit, but on fate (Moed Katan 28a). They have nothing to do with our good deeds or our merits. They are predetermined for us. But now is the time to pray for everything that seems locked and stuck.

When the high priest enters the Holy of Holies on Yom Kippur, he prays for each of these four keys. He walks with a rope affixed to his ankle. If, heaven forbid, he should die, he would be pulled out by the rope. He has time to offer only a short prayer, and so every word is critical, as the Talmud teaches:

> The High Priest would recite a brief prayer in the outer chamber.

What would he pray?

Ravin bar Adda and Rava bar Adda both say in the name of R. Yehuda:

May it be Your will, Lord our God, that this year shall be rainy and hot….

Rav Acha son of Rava, in the name of R. Yehuda, concluded: May the rule of power not depart from the House of Judah. And may Your nation Israel not depend upon each other for sustenance, nor upon another nation. (Taanit 24b)

This prayer refers to the key to rain (which is what travelers would pray for), the key to livelihood (so that the people of Israel need not be dependent on one another), and the key for the revival of the dead (which relates to the redemption associated with the House of Judah). The fourth key, which is about childbirth, is mentioned in a liturgical poem recited as part of the *Avoda* service, where we are told that the high priest prayed for "a year in which no woman will miscarry the fruit of her womb."

Each year, prior to Yom Kippur, I jot down a few words in pencil in my Yom Kippur prayer book. Next to the

271

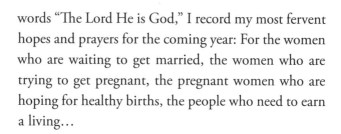

words "The Lord He is God," I record my most fervent hopes and prayers for the coming year: For the women who are waiting to get married, the women who are trying to get pregnant, the pregnant women who are hoping for healthy births, the people who need to earn a living...

And each year I am awed by the miracles that take place during these final moments of the Yom Kippur prayers. I look down at the names I scribbled in my prayer book the year before, and I marvel at the woman who has since been healed, the woman who has finally had a child...

In one more minute, the gate will be locked. It is almost time for the shofar blasts. Get your foot in the door before God seals your fate. Focus your heart and your tears on the verse from the Song of Songs: "Set me as a seal upon your heart, as a seal upon your arms, for love is as fierce as death" (Song of Songs 8:6). Proclaim your love to God. Pray that we remain sealed in the hearts of one another, and that we remain in this place of purity so that God might always love us just as fiercely.

And then the shofar is sounded and we part from God. "God has ascended amid shouts of joy, the Lord amid the sounding of the shofar" (Ps. 47:6). God will not be so close with us or so accessible to us until the following Elul. God will see and hear everything, but from a distance. The gates of "immediately" and "instantaneously" will be locked until next year. It will be a long time before we stand together in prayer with the fervor and urgency of this day.

The Rebbe of Kobryn (1783–1858) writes that a person might feel a bit crowded in synagogue on Yom Kippur, because the sanctuary is also populated by the souls of all the dead relatives of the members of the congregation. These souls stand before the holy ark and plead with God to have mercy on us and to grant us life. And so every person must pray with tears and with fervor, and repent wholeheartedly before God.

When the souls of the dead hear the sound of the shofar, they ask one another: Could that be the shofar heralding the redemption? Perhaps it is the shofar announcing the Messiah and the revival of the dead?

Rabbi Alexander Ziskind urges us to steal a glance beyond the closing gate. It is still open a tiny crack, and redemption lies just beyond.

I believe with all my heart in the redemption of this nation, whose people are so good. I meet them in the streets, at conferences, and at lectures. I meet such wonderful women – religious, secular, Lithuanian, hasidic, Mizrachi, Ashkenazic, *charedi*…. I am in awe of how they care for and look out for one another. As we recite in the *Avinu Malkeinu* prayer, "May this be an hour of mercy and divine favor before You." Master of the Universe, may our cries rise up before You. May we all be like prayer leaders in Your eyes. We have acted before You in accordance with this order. Now forgive us.

Our Father, our King,
inscribe us in the book of good life.

About the Author

Rabbanit Yemima Mizrachi is a renowned author, teacher, and inspirational speaker. Since 2001, she has given weekly lectures in Jerusalem that are now attended by thousands of women of all ages and affiliations, and her classes are disseminated virtually throughout the world. An attorney and rabbinical court advocate by training, Rabbanit Yemima speaks about a wide variety of topics: the weekly parasha, faith, prayer, marriage and relationships, family, holidays, and more. She also hosts a weekly program on Kan, Israel's public radio station.

Acknowledgements

Production editor: Reuven Ziegler
Assistant editor: Shira Finson
Copy editor: Debbie Ismailoff
Typesetting: Rina Ben Gal
Cover design: Eliyahu Misgav and Avigail Cohen
Internal design: Eliyahu Misgav and Tani Bayer

The fonts used in this book are from the Garamond family

Maggid Books
The best of contemporary Jewish thought from
Koren Publishers Jerusalem Ltd.